SCRIPTURE AND WORSHIP

BIBLICAL INTERPRETATION AND THE DIRECTORY FOR PUBLIC WORSHIP

RICHARD A. MULLER
and
ROWLAND S. WARD

D1527339

P&R
PUBLISHING
P.O. BOX 817 • PHILLIPSBURG • NEW JERSEY 08865-0817

Printed in the United States of America

Library of Congress Cataloging-in-Publication Data

Muller, Richard A. (Richard Alfred), 1948–
  Scripture and worship : biblical interpretation and the directory for
public worship / Richard A. Muller and Rowland S. Ward.
      p. cm. — (The Westminster Assembly and the Reformed faith)
  Includes bibliographical references and index.
  ISBN-13: 978-1-59638-072-1 (pbk.)
  1. Westminster Confession of Faith. 2. Presbyterian Church—Doctrines.
3. Reformed Church—Doctrines. 4. Public worship. I. Ward, Rowland S.,
1945– II. Title.
  BX9183.M85 2007
  230'.51—dc22
                                        2007018471

SCRIPTURE
AND
WORSHIP

THE WESTMINSTER ASSEMBLY AND THE REFORMED FAITH

A Series

CARL R. TRUEMAN

Series Editor

Contents

v

Series Introduction

The last two decades have seen a revolution in the way in which scholars have come to understand the nature and development of Reformed theology in the sixteenth and seventeenth centuries. It was in this context, and to further this scholarly revolution, that Westminster Theological Seminary in Philadelphia established the Craig Center for the Study of the Westminster Standards in 2002. The center provides a forum for promoting scholarly study of the history and theology of the Westminster Assembly, the various documents that it produced, and the way in which these documents have been received and used over the years.

As part of this project, the Craig Center has joined forces with P&R Publishing Company to commission a series of books, including monographs and collections of essays, that reflect this agenda. Each volume stands within the trajectories set by this new scholarship and takes seriously the theological content of Reformed orthodoxy while not naively divorcing that content from its historical or ecclesiastical context. Yet in doing this, these books do not become simply examples of antiquarianism or historicism. In fact, our desire is that this approach will free the past from the shackles and constraints of the agendas of the immediate present and thus allow voices from history to speak meaningfully to the world of today. It is thus the hope of the Craig Committee that both church and academy will benefit from this series for many years to come.

Carl R. Trueman
Chair of the Craig Committee

Preface

In 2004, Westminster Theological Seminary celebrated its seventy-fifth birthday by hosting a conference on the documents that stand at the very heart of Westminster's identity: the so-called Westminster Standards, consisting of the Westminster Confession, the Larger and Shorter Catechisms, and the Directory for Public Worship. These documents were the result of the work of the Westminster Assembly, convened by the English Parliament in 1643 in order to further the reformation of the Church of England; and, ever since, they have been the benchmark confessional standards of Presbyterian churches the world over.

Yet, for all of their worldwide significance, the documents are rarely understood, being variously regarded as the result of shallow proof-texting, of the over-systematization of doctrine, of logic-chopping, and of plain theological ignorance; and at the heart of such views lies a basic failure to understand the documents first and foremost as seventeenth-century productions that need to be understood within the context of the politics, theology, scholarship, and pedagogy of the time.

For this reason, the committee of the Craig Center for the Study of the Westminster Standards decided that there could be no better way to celebrate Westminster Theological Seminary's seventy-fifth birthday than by sponsoring a conference that would make a significant contribution to the necessary reassessment of the Westminster Standards in terms of their origin and construction within the seventeenth century. Thus, the committee was delighted when Dr. Richard A. Muller and Dr. Rowland S. Ward agreed to be the plenary speakers and to address the issues of the exegetical background to the confession (Dr. Muller) and the debates surrounding the writing of the Directory for Public Worship (Dr. Ward). Those papers have now been revised for publication, and they are what form the main text of the book you have before you.

It is the hope of the Craig Committee not only that this small volume will offer the careful reader a model of how the study of historical theological documents should be done, but also that it will rekindle interest in the Westminster Standards as part of the church's great creedal and confessional tradition.

Carl R. Trueman

PART 1

SCRIPTURE AND THE WESTMINSTER CONFESSION

Richard A. Muller

1

The "Whole Counsel of God": Scripture, Exegesis, and Doctrine in the *English Annotations* and the Westminster Confession

The *English Annotations* and the Westminster Standards

As has been noted by an increasingly large group of revisionist scholars, the theological pronouncements of the Reformed orthodox stand in a high degree of continuity with the theological intentions and with the specific pronouncements of the Reformers. This revisionist scholarship, with particular reference to the Westminster Standards, has been formulated over against a relatively sizable body of writings that have seen the confessions and catechisms as a rejection, distortion, or departure from the thought of the Reformers. One of the most fruitful ways of analyzing the continuities and commonalities, as well as the discontinuities and nuances of divergence and difference, between the Reformers and the writings of the Reformed orthodox or Puritan writers is to examine trajectories of exegesis—specifically to chart the rise of orthodoxy in and through the developing Reformed exegetical tradition.

As to the focus of the present essays, comparative examination of the two sets of normative documents commissioned by the Long

Parliament, namely, first, the exegetical and interpretive conclusions embodied, for public use, in the *Annotations upon all the books of the Old and New Testament*, best identified, in short form, as the *English Annotations*, and, second, the doctrinal standards embodied as the Westminster Confession of Faith and its accompanying catechisms affords, among other things, a unique and highly significant window into the relationships between biblical interpretation and theological formulation and to the continuities and discontinuities in religious thought that belong to the development of the Reformed tradition in the eras of the Reformation and of Protestant orthodoxy as that tradition moved from its beginnings into its era of confessionalization or institutionalization.

There was, however, no official relationship between the *English Annotations* and the Westminster Standards. It was not the case that the Parliament first commissioned a set of official annotations and then commissioned the Westminster Assembly to write a confession and catechisms based primarily on the reading of Scripture found in the *English Annotations*. Indeed, one of the eminent members of the Assembly, Cornelius Burgess, protested explicitly against such an association of the documents. "It is indeed true," he wrote,

> that some Members of that *Assembly*, joyning with some others, did compile some *Annotations upon the Bible*; which many take to be the work of the *Assembly*. But take this for an undoubted truth, those *Annotations* were never made by the Assembly, nor by any Order from it; nor after they were made had the *Approbation* of the Assembly; or were so much as offered to the Assembly at all, for that purpose or any other.[1]

His point, of course, was not to undermine the quality of the *Annotations*, but rather to take issue with his opponent, who had claimed that the Westminster Assembly approved of the gift of lands to the church on the basis of a particular annotation. Burgess, accordingly, and correctly, argued against the association of the *English Annotations* with the Westminster Assembly and its work.

1. Cornelius Burgess, *No Sacrilege nor Sin to purchase Bishops Lands*, 2nd ed. cap. iv, 87–88.

Much the same caveat concerning the *Annotations* carries over into Edmund Calamy's account of the era:

> There is one Work unjustly Ascribed to this *Assembly*, and that is the *Annotations on the Bible*, which commonly bear their Name. It is true, as is hinted in the Preface before the said Notes, the same Parliament that call'd the *Assembly*, employ'd the Authors of those Annotations: For Letters were directed to them by the Chairmen of the Committee for Religion, urging their Undertaking of that Work: And they were by Order of that Committee furnish'd with whatsoever books were needful. It is also true, That several of those that were concern'd in it, were Members of the Assembly: And yet it was not undertaken by the Directions or with the Consent of the Assembly; nor were the major Part Members of the Assembly: nor did any of the Assembly review the work when it was finished: So that it cannot, upon any Account, be said to be theirs.[2]

The *Annotations* and the confessional standards were thus parts of a larger parliamentary project for the stabilization of religion in England.

The *English Annotations*, completed in a first edition (1645) in the same year that the Westminster Assembly began its work on a new confession, provide a highly proximate index to the understanding of Scripture behind the doctrinal definitions and the biblical proofs found in the confession and catechisms.[3] The proximate location of the *Annotations* is enhanced, moreover, by the presence of several eminent members of the Assembly in the group of scholars gathered to compose the *Annotations*. The kind of continuities that exist between the confessional formulae and the teachings of the Reformers appear, moreover, not merely as parallels between the formal doctrines of the sixteenth- and seventeenth-century Reformed or developments of doctrinal formulae along the various trajectories of discussion and debate

---

2. Edmund Calamy, *An Abridgement of Mr. Baxter's History of His Life and Times. With an Account of the Ministers, &c. who were Ejected after the Restauration, of King Charles II*, 2nd ed., 2 vols. (London: John Lawrence, 1713), 1:86.

3. *Annotations upon all the books of the Old and New Testament wherein the text is explained, doubts resolved, Scriptures parallelled and various readings observed by the joynt-labour of certain learned divines, thereunto appointed, and therein employed, as is expressed in the preface* (London: John Legatt and John Raworth, 1645).

leading out of the Reformation, but as deeper continuities relating to the close understanding of the text and meaning of Scripture itself.

Scripture, Annotation, and Confession: Biblical Interpretation and the Formation of Doctrine in Seventeenth-Century England

The *Annotations* embody the text of the Authorized Version of Scripture and offer interpretations of that text that relate both to issues of translation and to issues of interpretation—in each case reflecting trajectories of discussion that had arisen at the beginnings of the Reformation and had continued in the Protestant tradition of biblical interpretation. Thus, by way of illustration of the purely textual issue, the text of the AV carried forward elements of the Tyndale-Coverdale-Rogers understanding of the biblical text (with its strong continental and frequently Lutheran accents), as well as elements of the sometimes different Geneva Bible (with its Calvinian and Bezan accents). In this context, it must be noted, a "Bezan accent" does not at all indicate, in the rather tendentious parlance of many nineteenth- and twentieth-century discussions of later Calvinism, a speculative predestinarianism—rather, it indicates the reliance of the Geneva Bible and its marginal apparatus on the eminent philological work of Beza in his own *Annotationes in Novum Testamentum*. Similarly, the phrases "Lutheran accent" and "Calvinian accent" indicate the exegetical results of the Reformers in their work of translating and interpreting the text of Scripture. I should also note here that the term "precritical," as applied to the older traditions of exegesis in the standard usage in the field, has a purely historical implication: it does not mean uncritical or non-text-critical, but only indicates the patterns and models of exegesis before the rise of the so-called historical-critical method.

First, to illustrate the point regarding translation: there are places in the *Annotations* where the nominally Genevan reading of a text in the AV has been juxtaposed with an interpretation that affirms the rather different understanding of the text found in the Tyndale-Coverdale-Rogers versions. For example, Hosea 6:7, both in the Geneva Bible and in the AV, reads, "Like man they transgressed the covenant." But the AV adds in the margin, "Heb. *like Adam*," indicating the Tyndale-Coverdale-Rogers tradition, and echoing both the Bishops' Bible and the typical continental readings. At this point the *English Annotations* accept the margin as the correct reading, disagreeing with both the Geneva Bible and the AV line: this text is, as far as all editions of the *Annotations* are concerned, a reference to Adam's violation of the covenant of works.

Second, and equally importantly, beyond the issue of the Protestant translation tradition, the *Annotations* drew on earlier interpretive decisions belonging to the precritical tradition of exegesis, looking to the earlier work of earlier commentators, and reaching back into the past of the church. There are, of course, no citations of older commentaries in the *Annotations*, so that the continuities with earlier understandings of Scripture are not overtly stated—yet the use, by the English annotators, of the Geneva Bible and its marginal commentary, of Tremellius's and Junius's marginal notes to their eminent Latin version, of the annotations of Johannes Piscator and those of Jean Diodati, and perhaps of the annotations to the Dutch *Statenvertaling* signal the presence of an interpretive tradition reaching back through these documents (and through other commentaries known and used by the English annotators) into the older exegetical tradition, not only of the Reformers but of the medieval commentators and of the church fathers. The nature of this continuity is important to note: it is not the rather flat, unvariegated identity confused with continuity and demanded as an ahistorical index of theological legitimacy by the proponents of the "Calvin against the Calvinists" perspective; rather, it is a highly nuanced and variegated continuity of dialogue and debate within which broad lines of development, specific issues of interpretation identified with trajectories of reading particular texts, and a fair degree of diversity within identifiable theological and confessional boundaries can be discerned. For example, one can identify lines of interpretation of particular texts that move through the precritical tradition, are fastened on by Calvin, lodged in the Geneva Bible, maintained by Diodati, and drawn over into the *English Annotations*—and one can also identify lines of interpretation that link the *Annotations*, perhaps by way of the *Statenvertaling*, perhaps by way of the older English tradition running from Tyndale through the Bishops' Bible, to non-Calvinian continental understandings of particular texts.

The extent to which the authors of the Westminster Standards defined their doctrinal formulae in relation to such traditions, as embodied for them in the work of the English annotators and other commentaries of the era, shows that they stood in a distinct continuity with the Reformation—not, of course, a flat, unnuanced continuity of stasis or identity of thought. Thus, the study of the doctrinal formulations in the Westminster Confession in the light of its context—with some emphasis on the exegetical context—offers opportunity not only for a presentation of the doctrine but, more importantly, for a contextualized reading of its theology, indicating on the one hand the continuity of its teaching with that of the Reformers and the Reformed confessions of the sixteenth century and, on the other, the continuity of the confession and its teaching with the developing thought of scholastic orthodoxy on the continent of Europe as well as among the British Reformed. The argument of this essay, thus, counters some of the claims that the confession represented a form of orthodox Protestantism that had strayed from the biblical theology of the Reformers and had replaced exegesis with dogmas.[4] It also, more generally, counters the rather ahistorical claims of some that the Westminster Confession represents a pre-scholastic phase of British Reformed or Presbyterian thought capable of being contrasted with the scholastic orthodoxy of the Continental writers of the same era—noting both the arrival in Britain of the scholastic mode of teaching and presenting theology a long generation before the writing of the confession, and the common ground and interrelationship between the British writers and the Continent, whether before, during, or after the writing of the

4. E.g., Holmes Rolston III, *John Calvin versus the Westminster Confession* (Richmond: John Knox, 1972); idem, "Responsible Man in Reformed Theology: Calvin Versus the *Westminster Confession*," *Scottish Journal of Theology* 23 (1970): 129–56; James B. Torrance, "Strengths and Weaknesses of the Westminster Theology," in *The Westminster Confession in the Church Today*, ed. Alisdair Heron (Edinburgh: Saint Andrews Press, 1982), 40–53; and idem, "Covenant or Contract? A Study of the Theological Background or Worship in Seventeenth-Century Scotland," *Scottish Journal of Theology* 23 (1970): 51–76.

confession.[5] This latter point also stands in the way of various attempts to read the thought of the English Puritans in a rather insular manner, despite the Puritans' own consistent intellectual commerce with the doctrinal, exegetical, and philosophical currents of Continental thought and the high profile and wide currency of various British writers (such as Perkins, Ames, Cameron, Rutherford, Twisse, and Owen) on the Continent. The context for understanding the Westminster Confession is, certainly, the exegetical and doctrinal heritage of the Reformation as presented through the interpretive glass of the English and Scots Reformed theology of the mid–seventeenth century,[6] which was itself part of the larger phenomenon that has been called "international Calvinism."[7]

Given both the doctrinal scope of the Westminster Standards (all of Christian doctrine in confessional and catechetical form) and the scope as well as size of the *English Annotations* (an exegesis of the entire Bible, in two volumes, over twenty-four hundred folio pages in length in the final edition), any study of the *Annotations* in relation to the confessional documents will need to be carefully limited. I propose to offer in the following essays an introduction to the *English*

---

5. Contra Jack B. Rogers, *Scripture in the Westminster Confession: A Problem of Historical Interpretation for American Presbyterianism* (Grand Rapids: Eerdmans, 1967); idem, "The Church Doctrine of Biblical Authority," in *Biblical Authority*, ed. Jack Rogers (Waco, Texas: Word Books, 1977), 17–46; idem, "The Authority and Interpretation of the Bible in the Reformed Tradition," in *Major Themes in the Reformed Tradition*, ed. Donald K. McKim (Grand Rapids: Eerdmans, 1992), 51–65; also Jack B. Rogers and Donald K. McKim, *The Authority and Interpretation of the Bible: An Historical Approach* (San Francisco: Harper and Row, 1979).

6. On this broader context, see Richard A. Muller, *Post-Reformation Reformed Dogmatics*, 4 vols. (Grand Rapids: Baker Book House, 2003); also note idem, *After Calvin: Studies in the Development of a Theological Tradition* (New York: Oxford University Press, 2003). The history of English religious thought during the sixteenth and seventeenth centuries was well surveyed in John Hunt, *Religious Thought in England from the Reformation to the End of the Last Century: A Contribution to the History of Theology*, 3 vols. (London: Strahan, 1870–73). On Scottish theology in the sixteenth and seventeenth centuries, see John Macleod, *Scottish Theology in Relation to Church History since the Reformation* (Edinburgh: Free Church of Scotland, 1943); and G. D. Henderson, *The Burning Bush: Studies in Scottish Church History* (Edinburgh, 1957). T. F. Torrance, *Scottish Theology: From John Knox to John McLeod Campbell* (Edinburgh: T. & T. Clark, 1996), is so tendentious and anachronistic in its theological judgments as to be without value as a historical study.

7. William Robert Godfrey, "Tensions within International Calvinism: The Debate on the Atonement at the Synod of Dort, 1618–1619" (PhD diss., Stanford University, 1974); and Menna Prestwich, ed., *International Calvinism, 1541–1715* (Oxford: Oxford University Press, 1985).

Annotations in their three editions (1645, 1651, and 1657), and two supplemental volumes (1655 and 1658); a chapter on the doctrine of Scripture and its interpretation in the Westminster Confession of Faith;[8] and a study of some selected doctrinal issues from the confession and catechisms that illustrate the relationship between the various biblical proofs cited by the Westminster Standards and the interpretive tradition evidenced in the *Annotations*.

8. This essay appeared in an earlier form as " 'The Only Way of Man's Salvation': Scripture in the Westminster Confession," in *Calvin Studies VIII: The Westminster Confession in Current Thought*, papers presented at the Colloquium on Calvin Studies (Davidson College, January 26–27, 1996), 14–33.

2

"An Entire Commentary . . . the Like Never Before Published in English": Annotating the Scriptures in the Era of the Westminster Assembly

The Task: Annotating the Authorized Version

The *Annotations upon all the books of the Old and New Testament*, first published in 1645, are reasonably well known among students of seventeenth-century Puritan and Reformed theology; but they have been little studied, whether historically, exegetically, or theologically.[1] The commentary has been referred to as the *Westminster Annotations* or the *Assembly's Annotations* because of the number of Westminster divines who participated in its compilation—in point of fact, however, the commentary was commissioned by the Long Parliament in 1640, well in advance of the calling of the Assembly (1643), as a British counterpart to the annotations to the Geneva Bible and the *Statenvertaling*. In the mid–seventeenth century, within a year of the first edition, the most common short form of reference to the work had become "English Annotations," probably to distinguish them from the running commentary on the *Statenvertaling*, which had become known in England as the "Dutch Annotations."[2]

1. The sole essay known to me is Dean George Lampros, "A New Set of Spectacles: The *Assembly's Annotations*, 1645–1657," *Renaissance and Reformation* 19 no.4 (1995): 33–46.
2. Cf. George Gillespie, *Aaron's Rod Blossoming. Or, the Divine Ordinance of Church Government Vindicated* (London: E. G. for Richard Whitaker, 1646), 1:iii, vii, x (pp. 20, 68, 97), with Robert Baillie, *The Letters and Journals of Robert Baillie, A.M. Principal of the University of Glasgow*, edited from the author's manuscripts by David Laing, 3 vols. (Edinburgh, 1841), 2:22, 167.

The task was delegated to a select group of exegetes and theologians called together by the parliamentary committee itself and comprising some divines who would later participate in the Assembly, and others who for various reasons would not—all identified for their exegetical and theological skills. The actual title of the work in its first edition of 1645 was *Annotations upon all the books of the Old and New Testament, wherein the text is explained, doubts resolved, Scriptures parallelled, and various readings observed by the joynt-labour of certain learned divines.*[3] A second edition followed in 1651,[4] a set of additional augmentations in 1655,[5] a full third edition in 1657,[6] and a volume of further annotations in 1658.[7] The magnitude of the task is worth noting in brief: in the first edition, the text exceeded 900 folio pages—by 1657, the annotators had more than trebled the content to the total of some 2,400 folio pages in two volumes, Genesis to the Song of Songs and Isaiah to the Revelation.

Nor were these the only sets of major annotations to the text of the Bible circulated during the era. The Geneva Bible, with its marginal notes, had remained widely available despite royal efforts to suppress

3. *Annotations upon all the books of the Old and New Testament wherein the text is explained, doubts resolved, Scriptures parallelled and various readings observed by the joynt-labour of certain learned divines, thereunto appointed, and therein employed, as is expressed in the preface* (London: John Legatt and John Raworth, 1645).

4. *Annotations upon all the books of the Old and New Testament this second edition so enlarged, as they make an entire commentary on the sacred Scripture: the like never before published in English: wherein the text is explained, doubts resolved, scriptures parallelled, and various readings observed / by the labour of certain learned divines thereunto appointed, and therein employed as is expressed in the preface,* 2 vols. (London: John Legatt, 1651).

5. John Richardson, *Choice Observations and Explanations upon the Old Testament . . . To which are added some further Observations upon the Whole Book of Genesis* (London: T. R. and E. M., 1655).

6. *Annotations upon all the books of the Old and Nevv Testament this third, above the first and second, edition so enlarged, as they make an entire commentary on the sacred scripture: the like never before published in English. Wherein the text is explained, doubts resolved, scriptures parallel'd, and various readings observed; by the labour of certain learned divines thereunto appointed, and therein employed, as is expressed in the preface,* 2 vols. (London: Evan Tyler, 1657).

7. *Additional annotations or, A collection of all the several additions to the third (above the first and second) impression of that most excellent work, intituled, annotations upon all the books of the old and new testament. By the labour of certain learned divines, thereunto appointed, by authority of Parliament. Published for the ease and benefit of th[ose] [w]ho have already bought the former impressions; with directions at the end of the preface, for the more ready finding where these additions should be inserted in the greater volume, to supply what is wanting therein* (London: Evan Tyler, 1658).

it.[8] English presses also released a stream of new editions of the New Testament based on Beza's Latin annotated translation as augmented by annotations of Junius on the Revelation,[9] translations of Diodati's Italian and French annotations,[10] and the *Dutch Annotations* arising out of the Synod of Dort.[11] Several English authors had also put forth large-scale annotations—notably, John Mayer,[12] Edward Leigh,[13] John Trapp,[14] and Henry Hammond.[15] With the exception of the *Dutch Annotations*, first published in translation in 1657, the same year as

8. In the margins of *The Bible and Holy Scriptures conteyned in the Olde and Newe Testament. Translated according to the Ebrue and Greke, and conferred with the best translations in diuers languages. With moste profitable annotations upon all the hard places* (Geneva, 1560), and subsequent editions.

9. E.g., *The New Testament of our Lord Iesus Christ, translated out of the Greeke by* Theod. Beza ... Englished by L. Tomson (London: Robert Barker, 1607); hereinafter cited as *New Testament* [Beza-Tomson].

10. Jean Diodati, *Pious Annotations upon the Holy Bible expounding the difficult places thereof learnedly, and plainly: with other things of great importance by the reverend, learned and godly divine, Mr. Iohn Diodati* (London: T. B. for Nicholas Fussell, 1643); *Pious and learned annotations upon the Holy Bible: plainly expounding the most difficult places thereof: also a methodicall analysis upon severall books of the Old and New Testament, setting down the chiefe heads contain'd therein: a worke not before this extant in English by Mr. John Diodati, the second edition, corrected and much enlarged: with additionall notes of the same author throughout the whole work* (London: Miles Flesher for Nicholas Fussell, 1648); third edition, further enlarged (London, 1651).

11. *The Dutch Annotations upon the Whole Bible: Or, All the holy canonical Scriptures of the Old and New Testament . . . as . . . appointed by the Synod of Dort, 1618, and published by authority, 1637,* trans. Theodore Haak, 2 vols. (London, 1657).

12. John Mayer, *A Commentarie upon the New Testament. Representing the divers expositions thereof, out of the workes of the most learned , both ancient Fathers, and moderne Writers,* 3 vols. (London, 1631); idem, *A Commentary upon all the Prophets both Great and Small: wherein the divers Translations and Expositions both Literal and Mystical of all the most famous Commentators both Ancient and Modern are propounded* (London, 1652).

13. Edward Leigh, *Annotations upon all the New Testament philologicall and theologicall wherein the emphasis and elegancie of the Greeke is observed, some imperfections in our translation are discovered, divers Jewish rites and customes tending to illustrate the text are mentioned, many antilogies and seeming contradictions reconciled, severall darke and obscure places opened, sundry passages vindicated from the false glosses of papists and hereticks* (London: W. W. and E. G. for William Lee, 1650); and idem, *Annotations on five poetical books of the Old Testament (viz.) Job, Psalmes, Proverbs, Ecclesiastes, and Canticles* (London: A. M. for T. Pierpoint, E. Brewster, and M. Keinton, 1657).

14. John Trapp, *A Commentary or Exposition upon . . . Proverbs of Solomon, Ecclesiastes, the song of songs, Isaiah, Jeremiah, Lamentations, Ezekiel & Daniel, Being a Third Volume of annotations upon the Whole Bible* (London, 1660).

15. Henry Hammond, *Deuterai phrontides, or, A review of the paraphrase & annotations on all the books of the New Testament: with some additions & alterations* (London: J. Flesher, 1656); idem, *A paraphrase and annotations upon all the books of the New Testament: briefly explaining all the difficult places thereof,* second edition corrected and enlarged (London: J. Flesher, 1659); idem, *A paraphrase and annotations upon the books of the Psalms, briefly explaining the difficulties thereof* (London: R. Norton, 1659).

the significantly larger third edition of the *Annotations*, all of these publications were selective in their method: they did not comment on the whole text but rather singled out specific points of interest, whether theological or philological. In addition, with the exception of the translation of Diodati—about which more will be said later—the *English Annotations* were the first to be printed entire, namely as a major one-volume Bible commentary.

The origin of the *English Annotations* is clear enough—as presented at length in the annotators' preface to the several editions, they arose as the result of an enquiry made in 1640 by the stationers and printers of London to the Committee for Religion of the House of Commons concerning the possibility of printing the text of the Authorized Bible of the day with a full set of annotations drawn from the Geneva Bible. The reason for the request was that the reading public, both clergy and lay, were understood as desiring an up-to-date annotated Bible.[16] The Geneva Bible, originally printed in 1560, had a set of detailed marginal annotations and had remained popular in the seventeenth century despite the ban placed on its British publication in 1616 by James I and Archbishop Laud. Import of the Bible from Dutch publishers was forbidden in 1630. By contrast, the Authorized Version of 1611, which had been licensed for publication by British printers, had no explanatory annotations, but only occasional marginal explanations of words by way of alternate translation, also by decree of James I. James had objected strenuously to the content of some of the Genevan annotations and, in accord with the policies of his royal predecessors, Henry VIII and Elizabeth I, viewed theological annotations in general with suspicion.

After the removal of press censorship in 1640, the stationers and printers sought to remedy the problem by continuing to publish the translation of the Bible that they had designed and set, but adding marginal annotations—specifically, merging the AV text with the *Geneva Annotations*. Some printings of these hybrid Bibles did in fact appear.[17]

16. *English Annotations*, fol. B4 recto; cf. the discussion in Lampros, "A New Set of Spectacles," 34–36.

17. E.g., *The Holy Bible containing the Old Testament and the New newly translated out of the originall tongues and with the former translations diligently compared and revised by His Majesties*

The committee recognized, however, a significant problem in the stationers, and printers, proposal: merging the *Geneva Annotations* with the AV text was less than desirable given that the Genevan annotations referenced a translation that was, in places, rather different from the Authorized Version. What is more, there had been dispute over some of the Genevan interpretations, and other of the annotations were viewed as incomplete or sketchy.[18] As the preface to the 1645 *Annotations* indicates, the committee licensed the printing of an annotated Bible, including in its license the specific order that there be a "review and correction of those [annotations] of the *Geneva* edition, by leaving out such of them, as there was cause to dislike, by clearing those that were doubtfull, and by supplying such as were defective."[19] The preface continues by noting, now from the annotators' perspective, that "Letters were directed to some of Us from the Chaire of the Committee for Religion, and personall invitations to others, to undertake and divide the Taske among Us."[20]

The Three Editions and the Scandal of the *Annotations*

The preface to the third edition offers a somewhat expanded version, from the perspective of the annotators, of their appointed task and of its alteration during the process of creating a new set of annotations. The annotations "were at first intended, as those before in the *Geneva* Version, for *Marginal Notes* onely affixed to the Text," and, in fact, parallel in form and size to those in the Geneva Bibles. The annotators consciously "constrained" their work, passing over "many things not unworthy otherwise of due observation and large discussion," in order that their annotations not take large portions of the printed page away from what had been "reserved for the [biblical] context."[21]

If the 1657 preface can be taken at face value on the issue, it appears that a complete or nearly complete set of annotations for publication in

---

speciall commandment, with most profitable annotations upon all the hard places and other things of great importance (Amsterdam: Joost Broerss, 1642).

18. *English Annotations* (1645), fol. B3 verso–B4 recto.
19. Ibid., fol. B4 recto.
20. Ibid.
21. *English Annotations* (1657), fol. ¶6 recto.

the margins of an edition of the AV was actually prepared and delivered, with some reservations concerning its brevity and its various omissions, to the parliamentary Committee for Religion. The committee, for its part, agreed with the annotators that a marginal apparatus like that of the Geneva Bible was in fact too abbreviated to fulfill their mandate for an annotated Bible. The preface continues, "Afterwards upon some second thoughts and further consideration, it seemed good unto those, who had put us upon this work, to alter their course at first propounded and publish the *Annotations* apart by themselves; the grounds of that former limitation and confinement both of Us and Them being now removed."[22]

The new instruction provides both an explanation of the "diversity for matter and dimension betwixt" the 1645 edition and the later revisions and of the rather diverse and varied character of the annotations in the 1645 edition itself. It appears that some of the annotators had followed the direction of the parliamentary committee quite closely and had produced only short annotations on the pattern of the Geneva Bible, whereas others had developed far longer annotations, some (like Gataker on Isaiah) actually writing out lengthy commentaries and then abridging them for use in the margins of the Bibles to be published. Given the new directions, those members of the group of annotators who had abridged or offered to abridge their larger commentaries "were then requested to lay that labour [namely, the abridgment] aside, and to let their Parts go entire as they were." The 1645 edition, hurried to press shortly after the decision to publish a separate commentary, included both forms of annotation—the longer commentaries and the more abbreviated, short forms, originally suited for the margins—leaving a volume that appeared, to many on the supervisorial committee and to many of the annotators themselves, inconsistent in its method.

According to the 1657 preface, the "other of [the annotators], who had held close to the former directions, would not have been unwilling accordingly to have enlarged, had . . . sufficient respite afforded for a fresh review and further supply of what might seem fit to adde unto the former."[23] In other words, the expansion of the

22. Ibid.
23. Ibid.

16

shorter annotations to match the depth and detail of the fuller commentary style also found in the original printing was not out of accord with the intentions of those who had initially produced only short annotations—not, at least, according to the editors of the later editions, although it appears unlikely that Pemberton was consulted by Richardson and Gataker when they vastly expanded the annotations on Ezekiel, Daniel, and the Minor Prophets.

As a note appended to the 1657 preface indicates, there had been a significant problem with Pemberton's annotations. On brief review, Pemberton's annotations on Ezekiel, Daniel, and the Minor Prophets can be counted among the short-form annotations in the 1645 edition. They were dwarfed, one might think embarrassingly so, by the vast work of Gataker on Isaiah, Jeremiah, and Lamentations that stood immediately before them. If their short compass had been their only problem, one might have imagined a Pembertonian expansion of the text for the next edition. After the publication of the *English Annotations*, however, a second edition of Diodati's *Annotations* appeared in English, with a rather sarcastic introductory notice "to the reader" by "R. G.," a self-confessed "well-affected Country-man" of the annotators, presumably the translator and editor of Diodati. So troublesome was the introductory notice that the annotators excerpted it and offered a brief rebuttal in their preface to the next edition.

R. G. had offered what he identified as three commendations of the value of Diodati's work. The first two were innocuous enough, both from divines who had praised the work prior to its translation, the first an unnamed "Reverend and eminent Divine now living in our Church," the second the "Learned Vedelius." The third, characterized in the note to the reader as "the most reall confirmation" of the three, was the implied recommendation of

> *Dr. Gouge, Mr. Gattaker, Mr. Downham, Mr. Ley, Mr. Reading, Mr. Taylor, Mr. Pemberton, and Dr. Featley,* who each of them taking a severall part of the Bible to make Annotations thereon, and printing them together in 1645, they all so highly approved of *Diodati's* Annotations, that anyone who shall please to compare those severall Notes of theirs, with the first Impression of this in English, shall finde many thousands of this our Authors [i.e., Diodati's] inserted, but

17

especially in *Ezekiel, Daniel,* and all the *minor Prophets,* where there is hardly any one Note of *Diodati's* forborn, but in theirs printed *verbatim* by our Translation: which had not their grave Wisdomes found both sound, acute, and pithy, I am confident they would never have made so great use thereof.[24]

Significant are both the broadside nature of the attack on the annotators and the rather specified comment indicating gross plagiarism in what was essentially Pemberton's work.

The annotators' response begins by noting that it is an "ancient practice . . . that savoreth rank of pride, and envy" to praise some persons by means of "false aspersions" and "unjust imputations" cast on others. In this case, R. G. has cast "a false and slandrous calumny on sundry Divines, eight of whom he nameth, & layes to the charge of every one of them" that they had composed their annotations by taking thousands of phrases wholesale out of Diodati. So much one could expect in response—but the implication, found between the lines of what follows in the annotators' rebuttal, is both unexpected and quite revealing:

> For Seven of the Eight, whom he names, let his own rule be observed; namely, their Notes compared with *Diodati's,* and the many thousands will not be found one. It may be that in some places they may agree with *Tremellius,* and *Junius,* with *Piscator,* and other Learned and Orthodox Annotators on the Old and New Testament, whom *Diodati* hath much traced, and thereupon all agree in the same Truth: but from thence to infer, that the Seven English Annotators have inserted *Diodati's* Notes into theirs, is so false an inference, as any *Sophister* would say, non sequitur.[25]

The annotators go on to state that their work had been completed and "given up to the Stationers" before the publication of the first English edition of Diodati—while proof of their independence could easily be seen in the fullness of their annotations, which had discussed many things not noted at all by Diodati and had "fully

---

24. Diodati, *Pious and Learned Annotations* (1651), fol. A3 verso; cf. *English Annotations* (1657), fol. ¶6 verso.
25. *English Annotations* (1657), fol. ¶6 verso.

cleared sundry difficulties" that Diodati himself had declared unre-solvable. The preface to the *Annotations*, thus, exonerates "Seven of the Eight"—leaving Pemberton, the eighth annotator, to borrow a phrase from a later era, to twist slowly in the wind.

And, indeed, whereas a quick perusal of various books throughout the divines' 1645 *Annotations* reveals occasional resemblances and, here and there, a few parallel phrases, the verbatim use of Diodati is more than obvious from the beginning of Ezekiel to the end of the Old Testament—as are Pemberton's omissions of most of the verses not interpreted by Diodati. His introductions to the various books or "Arguments" appear to be original. At least they do not duplicate Diodati.

There had been, in other words, a good deal of truth in the accusations of R. G. As a result both of the accusations and of the desire for a more methodologically uniform commentary, Mr. Pemberton's work was radically emended and augmented, without notice, in the second and third editions of the *English Annotations*. Still, it remains the case, even in the 1657 text, that many of the offending phrases may be found, nearly buried, in the mass of new material inserted by Richardson.[26] It should also be added—a point to which we shall return below—that the annotators continued to remain anonymous in their efforts despite the relative eminence of some of them as theologians and exegetes. Their intention had not been to produce an original work, but rather a standard commentary that drew on the already sizable and significant Reformed exegetical tradition.

The Annotators: The Scholars, Their Qualifications, and Their Achievements

The accusation brought by R. G. against the *Annotations* offered one of the contemporary listings of the contributors, naming "Dr. Gouge, Mr. Gattaker, Mr. Downham, Mr. Ley, Mr. Reading, Mr. Taylor, Mr. Pemberton, and Dr. Featley," eight divines in all. The response offered in the preface to the third edition of the *Annotations*

---

26. Cf. *English Annotations*, Ezekiel 1:1, 5, in loc., with Diodati, *Pious and Learned Annotations*, Ezek. 1:1, 5, in loc.

speaks of the "Eight." What is clear from other accounts, however, is that the mention of these eight divines was not an exhaustive accounting of the writers and that the annotators' response, speaking of the "Eight" and exonerating "Seven of the Eight," was a reference to R. G.'s list, not to the full number of the exegetes. The impression that one receives from the prefaces to the *Annotations*, moreover, is of a corporate endeavor in which the names of the individual annotators were not to be highlighted in any way. Thus, the title of the work, *Annotations upon all the books of the Old and New Testament wherein the text is explained, doubts resolved, Scriptures parallelled and various readings observed by the joynt-labour of certain learned divines, thereunto appointed, and therein employed, as is expressed in the preface*, consciously omits the names of the annotators and simply identifies them as "certain learned divines." The prefaces offer no further information—indeed, no personal information concerning the annotators at all.

The best accounting of the writers of the *Annotations* comes to us from Edmund Calamy the Younger—the son of the Westminster divine of the same name. It is the source for the listing that appears in Neal's *History of the Puritans* and Reid's *Memoirs of the Westminster Divines*.[27] The passage is worth quoting in its entirety from Calamy, if only to put aside the modifications introduced by the later writers into their paraphrases. After indicating that the *English Annotations* were in no way the work of the Westminster Assembly, Calamy continued:

> However, it was a good Work in its Season, and I shall add the names of the true Authors, as far as my best Enquiry would helpe me Intelligence. Mr *Ley*, Sub-Dean of *Chester*, did the *Pentateuch*. Dr. *Gouge* had the two Books of *Kings*, and *Chronicles*, *Ezra*, *Nehemiah* and *Esther* for his Province. Mr. *Meric Casaubon* did the *Psalms*. Mr. *Francis Taylor* the *Proverbs*, And Dr. *Reignolds*, *Ecclesiastes*. Mr. *Swalwood* who was recommended by *Archbishop Usher*, did *Solomon's*

27. James Reid, *Memoirs of the Lives and Writings of those Eminent Divines who Convened in the Famous Assembly at Westminster, in the Seventeenth Century*, 2 vols. (Paisley: Stephen and Andrew Young, 1811–15; repr. Edinburgh: Banner of Truth, 1982), 301–2; biographies of several of the contributors can also be found in Benjamin Brooke, *The Lives of the Puritans: Containing a Biographical Account of those Divines who Distinguished Themselves in the Cause of Religious Liberty from the Reformation under Queen Elizabeth, to the Act of Uniformity, in 1662*, 3 vols. (London: James Black, 1813; repr. Ligonier, PA: Soli Deo Gloria Publications, 1994).

Song. The Learned *Gataker* did *Isaiah, Jeremiah,* and *Lamentations:* And is (in the Opinion of many Competent Judges) exceeded by no Commentator, Antient or Modern, on these Books. *Ezekiel, Daniel,* and the small Prophets, were in the first Edition done by *Mr. Pemberton,* and in the Second by Bishop *Richardson.* The Notes on the four *Evangelists,* are Mr *Ley's,* and those on St. *Paul's* Epistles Dr. *Featley's;* which latter are broken and imperfect, on the Account of the Author's dying before he had revis'd or finish'd them. There were also two other Persons concern'd in this Work, *viz.* Mr. *Downame* and Mr. *Reading,* who might probably have the other Parts of Scripture allotted them, that are not here mention'd.[28]

From the title page and preface to the additional annotations of 1655, we can gather also that Richardson was their primary author, assisted by Gataker in the additional annotations on Genesis, with some assistance, also in the annotations on Genesis, from James Ussher. Downame is known as the compiler of the concordance to the Bibles of the era. Of these writers, Ley, Gouge, Taylor, Reynolds, Gataker, and Featley were members of the Westminster Assembly, leaving Casaubon, Pemberton, Richardson, Downame, Reading, Swalwood or Smallwood, and Ussher as writers not directly associated with the Assembly. Featley is remembered as the last of the Episcopalians to remain with the Assembly—Ussher, of course, was invited, but refused to attend. This accounting of the authors is, of course, incomplete—no mention is made of the annotator or annotators for Joshua through 2 Samuel, for Job, for the Acts, or for the Catholic Epistles and the Revelation. If, moreover, Hebrews was not included among the Pauline Epistles, its annotator is also unidentified.

Two things are remarkable, at least to the modern observer, about this list and the *Annotations*—on the one hand, the list was broadly constructed, drawing not only on the Presbyterian and independent constituencies of the Parliament that would be called together into the Westminster Assembly, but also on the Episcopalian and, indeed, Royalist constituency that would not contribute to the Assembly and

---

28. Edmund Calamy, *An Abridgement of Mr. Baxter's History of His Life and Times. With an Account of the Ministers, &c. who were Ejected after the Restauration, of King Charles II,* 2nd ed., 2 vols. (London: John Lawrence, 1713), 1:86.

its standards. In the latter group we count Ussher and Richardson, both bishops in Ireland; Featley, and Smallwood. On the other hand, the annotators remained anonymous in the published text: despite the eminence of many of the contributors, their names were not listed in the prefaces, nor were they affixed to the commentaries on the various books of the Bible.

Florence Estienne Meric Casaubon (1599–1671), son of the philologist, Isaac Casaubon; educated at Christ College, Oxford (BA, 1618; MA, 1621; DD, 1636); he held the livings of two parishes but appears to have devoted most of his time to study.

John Downham (1571–1652), otherwise Downame; educated in Christ's College, Cambridge (BA, 1593; MA, 1596; BD, 1603). He served as vicar of St. Olave Jewery, London, from 1599–1602; as rector of St. Margaret, Lothbury, 1602–18; and rector of All-Hallows-the-Great, 1630–52. From 1643 onward, he served as a licenser of the press and, although not a member of the Westminster Assembly, he served on the committee for the ordination of ministers. His chief works are *The Summe of Sacred Divinitie* (1630)[29] and *The Christian Warfare* (1604–12).

Daniel Featley (1582–1645) was educated at Corpus Christi College, Oxford; he served as chaplain to George Abbot, archbishop of Canterbury, and briefly was chaplain to Charles I. He was of both Episcopalian and Royalist sympathies, but also distinctly Reformed in his doctrine. As noted above, he was the author of the annotations on the Pauline Epistles, perhaps including the epistle to the Hebrews, but that is not certain. His credentials as an exegete are demonstrated in his *Mystica Clavis: A Key Opening . . . Holy Scripture.*[30] He also wrote an extended catechism and a noteworthy work on Christian piety, plus a series of major anti-Arminian essays.[31]

---

29. See my discussion of this document and its pedigree in Richard A. Muller, "Covenant and Conscience in English Reformed Theology: Three Variations on a Seventeenth Century Theme," *Westminster Theological Journal* 42, no. 2 (Spring 1980): 313.

30. Daniel Featley, *Mystica Clavis: a Key opening divers difficult and mysterious Texts of Scripture, in 70 Sermons* (London, 1636).

31. Daniel Featley, *The Summe of Saving Knowledge* (London: G. Miller, 1625); idem, *Ancilla pietatis, or the Handmaid to Private Devotion* (London, 1626); idem, *Parallelismus novantiqui erroris Pelagiarminiani* (London: Miles Flesher, 1626); idem, *A parallel: of nevv-old Pelgiarminian error* (London: Robert Milbourne, 1626); idem, *A second parallel* (London:

Thomas Gataker (1574–1654), one of the more eminent of the annotators, was characterized by his friend and contemporary Edward Leigh as "a solid, judicious, and pious Divine; as his divers learned Latine and English Treatises shew,"[32] and by others in his era as the most accomplished linguist and philologist among the Westminster divines.[33] Nor were his extensive annotations on Isaiah, Jeremiah, and Lamentations and his editorial work on the additional annotations on Genesis of 1655 his only biblical studies: he also wrote a major study of the biblical name of God, a second treatise on the same subject defending his conclusions against objectors, and perhaps his most famous work in his own time, the dissertation on the style and language of the New Testament, arguing both the historical development of the Greek language and the presence in the New Testament of Hebraisms and Syriasms.[34]

William Gouge (1575–1653) wrote the annotations on 1 Kings through Esther, and, in another account, those on Job as well.[35] His degrees—Bachelor of Arts, Bachelor of Divinity, and Doctor of Divinity—were from King's College, Cambridge. He was known for his vast knowledge of Scripture, his massive grasp of Hebrew, and his ability in logic and philosophy. He lectured on the latter two subjects at Cambridge. His other major exegetical achievement was his massive commentary on Hebrews.[36] Gouge also wrote an extensive commentary on Psalm 116.[37]

John Ley (1583–1662), the sub-dean of Cheshire and president of Sion College, Oxford, is typically credited with the authorship of

---

J. Haviland for Robert Milbourne, 1626); idem, *Pelagius redivivus. Or Pelagius raked out of the ashes by Arminius and his schollers* (London: Robert Mylbourne, 1626).

32. Edward Leigh, *A Treatise of Religion and Learning and of Religious and Learned Men*, 6 vols. (London: A. M. for Charles Adams, 1656), 5:i (205).

33. Cf. the citations in Reid, *Memoirs*, 1:308.

34. Thomas Gataker, *De nomine tetragrammato dissertatio* (London: R. Cotes, 1645); *Dissertatio de tetragrammato suae vindicatio adversus Capellum* (London: Roger Daniel, 1652); and *De novi instrumenti stylo dissertatio. Qua viri doctissimi Sebastiani Pfochenii, de lingue Gracae Novi Testamenti puritate; in qua Hebraismus, quae vulgo finguntur, quam plurimis larva detrahi dicitur* (London: T. Harper, 1648).

35. See Reid, *Memoirs*, 1:354; but note Reid, *Memoirs*, 1:302 and Brooke, *Lives*, 3:167, where Neal's account is followed.

36. William Gouge, *Commentary on Hebrews* (London, 1655).

37. William Gouge, *The Saints Sacrifice: Or, A Commentarie On the CXVI. Psalme. Which is, A Gratulatory Psalme, for Deliverance from deadly Distresse* (London: George Miller, 1632).

23

the *English Annotations* on the Pentateuch and the four Gospels.[38] Ley
studied at Christ's Church College, Oxford. His earliest and only other
exegetical publication was a defense of the marginal annotations to
the Geneva Bible.[39]

John Reading (1587/88–1667) was a graduate of Magdalen Hall,
Oxford (BA, 1607), and St. Mary Hall (MA, 1610). He was ordained
by the bishop of Oxford and served as chaplain to Edward la Zouche,
Lord Zouche, and later as chaplain-in-ordinary to Charles I. He may
have eventually received a BD. He is remembered as a strict Calvin-
ist, esteemed for his sermons—although his Royalist leanings led to
a brief imprisonment and deprivation of livelihood in 1644. He was
restored to his living following the Restoration.

Edward Reynolds (1599–1676), the annotator of Ecclesiastes,
wrote one other work in the genre of biblical commentary—a massive
examination of Psalm 110, running to 525 quarto pages.[40] Reynolds
was educated at Merton College, Oxford (BA, 1618; MA, 1624), and
served first as preacher at Lincoln's Inn (1622) and later as rector
of Braunston (1631). He was a moderate Presbyterian and member
of the Westminster Assembly. After the Restoration he advocated a
moderate episcopacy and was made bishop of Norwich in 1661.

John Richardson (1579/80–1654) was one of the first students
to graduate from Trinity College, Dublin (MA, 1601; BD, 1610;
DD, 1614). He served as a fellow of Trinity College and a preacher
in Dublin, offering lectures on the book of Isaiah as an associate of
James Ussher. He was made bishop of Ardagh in 1633.

Francis Taylor (1590–1656), who annotated the Proverbs, was
educated at Cambridge and was known in his time as, in the words
of Edward Leigh, "a learned Linguist,"[41] capable in Hebrew, Aramaic,
and Syriac as well as Greek and Latin. Among his works are a trans-

38. Calamy, *Abridgement . . . Account of the Ministers*, 1:86; Daniel Neal, *The history of the Puritans, or, Protestant non-conformists . . . with an account of their principles*, new edition, revised, corrected, and enlarged, by Joshua Toulmin, 5 vols. (Bath: R. Cruttwell, 1793–97), 3:453; Brooke, *Lives*, 3:403; Reid, *Memoirs*, 2:53–54.
39. John Ley, *An Apology in Defence of the Geneva Notes on the Bible* (London, 1612).
40. Edward Reynolds, *An Explication of the cx. Psalm* (London, 1632; 2nd ed. 1635; 3nd ed. 1642).
41. Leigh, *Treatise of Religion and Learning*, 6:i; noted also in Reid, *Memoirs*, 2: 179–81.

lation of the Jerusalem Targum into Latin, various rabbinic studies, and a lengthy exposition of Proverbs chapters 1 through 9, published independently of the *English Annotations*.[42]

Two of the annotators, identified only by last name as "Mr. Swalwood" or "Smallwood" and "Mr. Pemberton," are difficult to identify. We do not find any well-published exegetes or theologians of either name in the *Short-Title Catalogue*, and there appears to be no one named "Swalwood" at all, that form being either a variant or a typographical error for "Smallwood." There are two individuals with theological training named Smallwood who might be the annotator—one, Allan Smallwood, the author of a single published sermon; the other, Matthew Smallwood, the deceased owner of a library available for sale in 1684. The case for Matthew Smallwood, dean of Lichfield, as the author of the commentary on the Song of Songs is surely better than any case to be made for the otherwise unknown Allan Smallwood, but it is circumstantial at best. Of the several university-trained Smallwoods, he is certainly the one who most closely fits the profile of a biblical commentator, although, as far as the *Short-Title Catalogue* is concerned, he published nothing. He was also a Royalist and a proponent of episcopacy—but given the presence of Daniel Featley and John Richardson among the annotators, and James Ussher as an editorial consultant, this opposition to the policies of the Long Parliament would certainly not have been a condition for his exclusion from the group of annotators. There is also the collateral testimony provided by the auction catalogue of his library, in which one finds a concentration of works on the Song of Songs.[43]

In the case of Mr. Pemberton, however, the trail goes rather cold. The only published Pemberton noted by the *Short Title Catalogue* who lived at the time of the *Annotations* is Sir Francis Pemberton, the Chief Justice of the Court of Common Pleas—an unlikely candidate. Calamy mentions a Matthew Pemberton, the ejected minister of Clayhadon, Devonshire, afterwards a dissenting minister in Marlborough, but notes

42. Francis Taylor, *An Exposition of the First Nine Chapters of the Proverbs*, 2 vols. (London, 1655).

43. Cf. *Catalogus Librorum reverendi doctiq. Viri Matth. Smallwood, S. T. P., St. decani de Lychfield nuper defuncti* (London, 1684).

no writings except indicating his co-authorship with Thomas Vincent of a memorial sermon, *The Death of Ministers Improved*.[44] There is a host of various Pembertons in alumni lists of Oxford and Cambridge, but none steps to the fore. Given the nature of Mr. Pemberton's contribution to the first edition of the *English Annotations*, this relative anonymity may well be the most merciful conclusion.

The Exegetical Self-Understanding of the Annotators: The Tradition of Reform in Text and Annotation

As the preface indicates, the annotators understood themselves as belonging to a particular tradition of translation and interpretation. The full title of the preface explains that the annotators wish to "present some important considerations of the happy progresse of the Gospel in this Kingdom; together with an account of their undertaking and performance of this Service for the clearing of the Sacred Text to the understanding of the Christian Reader." The reformation of religion that had occurred during the century past was "almost miraculously wrought," although, the annotators add, "we professe to beleeve Gods Word, without the pawn of a miracle to make it good" against the "mightie Engines" of the pope and his minions.[45] In the presence of this great and continuing manifestation of the power of the Word, the annotators point to four issues that ought to be addressed in order to provide a suitable context for their work:

The first concerning Preachers, and preaching of the Word, and the administration of the Sacrament of the Lords Supper.

The second the Translation of the Scriptures into a tongue understood by the vulgar people.

The third of the necessitie and utility of Annotations, for the exposition of difficult places.

44. Edmund Calamy the Younger, *Nonconformist Memorial*, 2nd ed. (London, 1677), 1:346.
45. *English Annotations* (1545), fol. B1 recto.

26

The fourth, especiall considerations upon some Notes and Annotations in particular.[46]

The first point, concerning preachers and preaching, rehearses the dearth of sound preaching and the absence of sound training in theology prior to the Reformation, the use of the pulpit for the "locall exaltation," not of the Word, but of certain "priests . . . above the heads of the people." This "famine of the Word" was alleviated in the Reformation by a "greate company of Preachers" who spoke the Word in public. All effort must be made, the annotators continue, to prevail against plots to turn back the Reformation, plots designed to restrict preaching to the Sabbath only, to turn sermons into prepared standard homilies.[47] A second remedy to the restriction of the Word is the translation of Scripture "into a language understood by unlearned people, that they might *search the Scriptures*, and by searching of them might *finde in them*, what is most to be desired, *eternall life*; for they are Bookes not for the Clergie onely . . . but for the common people likewise, yea for women as well as men." Were this not so, Saint John "would not have written one of his epistles . . . to an elect Lady" and the "learned Doctor Hierome" would not have counseled mothers to teach Scripture daily to their daughters.[48] In order to emphasize the latter point, translation into the vernacular, the annotators next offer a history of the English translations of the Bible in whole and in part, beginning in the eighth century with the Saxon Psalms of Adelme of Sherborne and concluding with the publication of the Authorized Version in 1612.[49]

The public preaching and daily reading of Scripture cannot, of course, be the simple and sole solution to the problem of human need for words of salvation. The annotators pose the further question to "those who are daily conversant in the reading of the Bible, and read it by course, from the one end to the other," namely the question put by Philip to the eunuch, "Understandest thou what thou readest?"—the answer being, "How can I except, some man

46. Ibid., fol. B1 verso.
47. Ibid.
48. Ibid., fol. B2 recto.
49. Ibid., fol. B2 verso–B3 recto.

should guide me?" (Acts 8:30–31).[50] The resolution to the problem, the stable guide to the meaning of the text is, of course, the set of annotations:

> The third thing which improveth the price of our portion in Religion, is the necessary use and great benefit of Expositions and Annotations upon the Bible, to render the right meaning of the words of the Translation, as the Translation doth of the words of the Originall; for though the Scriptures may have their use, and force upon the affections of the ignorant Readers, at first sight, without any serious search into their hidden sense, and may have a work upon the Will to encline it to good, or withdraw it from evil . . . yet what *Peter* saith of his beloved brother *Pauls* Epistles, *there be some things which are hard to be understood,* 2 *Pet.* 3:15–16, may be truly said of many other parts of holy Scripture, especially in the books of *Genesis, Job, Canticles, Ezekiel, Daniel,* and the *Revelation.*[51]

Of course, no such guide is infallible and the best interpreter may sometimes be at a loss to explain a difficult text perfectly—"yet he may make such a probable interpretation . . . as may prevent a dangerous misconstruction of an imprudent inconsiderate Reader."[52]

After rehearsing the story of the decision to produce a new set of annotations and of the formation of their committee, the English annotators go on to clarify the nature of their efforts and the relation of their work to several sets of eminent earlier annotations, namely Diodati's *Italian Annotations,* the *Dutch Annotations* arising out of the Synod of Dort, and *Geneva Annotations.*[53] So also, in the case of the *Geneva Annotations,* the annotators indicate their respect for this revered running commentary and state that they view it as entirely orthodox, free from theological errors—yet they have worked as the "builders of a new house," not merely patching up an old edifice, but taking it down and replacing it with a new one. They then rather carefully note, already in 1645, prior to the plagiarism dispute, their

50. Ibid., fol. B3 recto–B3 verso.
51. Ibid., fol. B3 recto.
52. Ibid., fol. B3 verso.
53. Ibid., fol. B4 recto.

reliance on these previous expositions of the text. They have indeed used these texts,

> yet so, that if we have borrowed aught of either, as they have done of those, who did precede them, in the like Observations, we shall desire but to take it to usury, and to make our returne of what we receive, farre above the rate of ordinary interest: And in this holy businesse we have no other ambition than to give better satisfaction to an apprehensive Reader, for the sense of the whole Bible, then (in this kinde) we have met withall, in any one Worke of what Authors soever.[54]

In their method, therefore, they have followed the advice of the apostles, recognizing that no Scripture is "of private interpretation" (2 Peter 1:20) and also that "the spirits of the prophets are subject to the prophets" (1 Cor. 14:32)—accordingly, the "private dictates" of the annotators have been "submitted . . . to the censure and correction of [their] Colleagues in this Service daily assembled together, for the perusal of every ones part."[55] Clearly, then, there were borrowings: the new house was not erected out of entirely new brick and lumber—but the annotators not only assumed this background in the earlier tradition, both by their admission and explanation and by their anonymity, they refrained from taking personal credit for what they perceived to be the propounding, not of personal opinion, but of the results of an exegetical tradition of which they were a part. They also, as stated, compared and checked one another's work. Thus, the comment on Hosea 6:7, already noted, indicates, among other things, the conscious placement of the *Annotations* in a particular exegetical tradition—in the case of the first edition, simply taking Diodati's reading of the text and, by means of it, identifying with the older English and the majority continental tradition, as distinct from the generic reading found in Calvin, the Geneva Bible, and Tremellius.

54. Ibid.
55. Ibid., fol. B4 recto–verso.

3

"Inspired by God—Pure in All Ages": The Doctrine of Scripture in the Westminster Confession

The Assembly and the Confession

In July 1643, the Westminster Assembly met for the first time.[1] Barely a month later, Parliament went to war with the king—and the war, as much as the work of the Assembly, would determine the nature of religion in England. The Assembly itself consisted of an eminent body of British theologians and clergy together with a set of parliamentary delegates: originally there were 10 delegates from the House of Lords, 20 from the Commons, and 121 divines. Richard Baxter would later declare that "as far as I am able to judge by the information of all history of that kind, and by any other evidences left us, the Christian world, since the days of the apostles, had never a synod of more excellent divines than this and the synod

1. In addition to Benjamin Breckinridge Warfield, *Westminster Assembly and Its Work* (New York: Oxford University Press, 1931; repr. Grand Rapids: Baker Book House, 1981), the major studies and sources of the work of the Assembly remain William H. Hethrington, *The History of the Westminster Assembly of Divines*, (3rd ed., Edinburgh, 1856); Alexander F. Mitchell, *The Westminster Assembly: Its History and Standards* (London, 1883); Alexander F. Mitchell and John Struthers, eds., *The Minutes of the Sessions of the Westminster Assembly of Divines* (Edinburgh: William Blackwood, 1874).

of Dort."[2] Indeed, several members of the Westminster Assembly, notably, William Twisse (1575–1646), John Lightfoot (1602–75), and Thomas Gataker (1574–1654), were internationally renowned in their own time, and many of the other members had significant reputations in Britain as theologians and scholars.

The first order of business at the Westminster Assembly was a revision of the Thirty-nine Articles of the Church of England, specifically for the sake of preventing either an Arminian or a catholicizing reading. This work moved forward, and by October of 1643, the Assembly had in hand a revised text of the first fifteen of the Thirty-Nine Articles. By October, however, the war between king and Parliament had become difficult, and Parliament concluded an alliance with the Scots. The Solemn League and Covenant concluded between Parliament and the Scots radically altered the work of the Assembly. Inasmuch as the Solemn League and Covenant called for the closest "conjunction and uniformity" between the churches in Scotland and England, the Assembly now had to take up the task of a full religious reformation, relating to worship, discipline, and church government as well as doctrine. The Assembly spent the ten months following the Solemn League and Covenant preparing a directory of worship to replace the Book of Common Prayer.

Given the fact that the Scots had their own Reformation-era confession and were not inclined to accept a revision of the English Articles, and given the increasing sentiment that a full reformation was called for, the Assembly moved toward composing a totally new document. Indeed, the Scots, more than the English, had recognized, at the point of signing the Solemn League, that none of their older confessional documents were suitable to the purpose of union and that a new confession would be necessary.[3] On August 20, 1644, the Assembly returned to the work of drafting a confession and established "a Committee to join with the Commissioners of the Church of Scotland to prepare matter for a joint Confession of Faith." The committee consisted of William Gouge, Thomas Gataker, John Arrowsmith,

2. William Orme, *The Life and Times of Richard Baxter: with a Critical Examination of His Writings*, 2 vols. (London: James Duncan, 1830), 1:86.
3. See Warfield, *Westminster Assembly*, 54–55, citing letters of the Scots commissioner, Robert Baillie.

Thomas Temple, Jeremiah Burroughs, Cornelius Burges, Richard Vines, Thomas Goodwin, and Joshua Hoyle. On September 4, this initial committee reported to the Assembly and, on the specific request of the chair, Thomas Temple, asked that its number be augmented by the addition of Herbert Palmer, Matthew Newcomen, Charles Herle, Edward Reynolds, Thomas Wilson, Anthony Tuckney, Brocket (Peter) Smith, Thomas Young, John Ley, and Obadiah Sedgwick. The Assembly acceded to the additions.[4] Of this full committee, William Gouge, Thomas Gataker, and John Ley had also served as annotators of the Bible; there was, in other words, a personally significant (but not very large) overlap between the select group of annotators and the committee that produced the Westminster Confession of Faith.

In April 1645, after much delay on the part of the Assembly, the House of Commons formally instructed the Assembly to proceed with its work on the confession. On April 21, a committee—presumably not the committee organized to draft the new Confession of Faith— reported on the Thirty-nine Articles, recommending a review of the document. In response, the Assembly ordered this committee to determine which, if any, of the Articles should be considered "useful . . . till a Confession of Faith can be drawn up by this Assembly."[5] The committee on the Articles was to meet that day, and the committee on the new confession was called to meet on the following Wednesday—but it was only on May 12 that a somewhat reconstituted committee was finally named.[6] A first draft of the chapter on Scripture was written by the committee and presented for discussion and debate on July 7. Debate continued through July 18. At that time, three subcommittees were formed to deal with specific doctrinal

---

4. Mitchell and Struthers, *Minutes*, lxxxvii; *The Whole Works of the Rev. John Lightfoot, D. D. Master of Catharine Hall, Cambridge*, ed. John Rogers Pitman (13 vols. London: J. F. Dove, 1825), 305; for lives of the divines, see: James Reid, *Memoirs of the Lives and Writings of those Eminent Divines who Convened in the Famous Assembly at Westminster, in the Seventeenth Century* 2 vols. (Paisley: Stephen and Andrew Young, 1811–15; repr. Edinburgh: Banner of Truth, 1982); biographies of Arrowsmith, Temple, Gataker, Harris, Herle, Hoyle, and Whitaker are also found in Benjamin Brooke, *The Lives of the Puritans: Containing a Biographical Account of those Divines who Distinguished Themselves in the Cause of Religious Liberty from the Reformation under Queen Elizabeth, to the Act of Uniformity, in 1662*, 3 vols. (London: James Black, 1813; repr. Ligonier, PA: Soli Deo Gloria Publications, 1994).
5. Mitchell and Struthers, *Minutes*, 83.
6. Ibid., 91.

topics.[7] After a year of work, on September 25, 1646, the first nineteen chapters of the confession were delivered to the House of Commons for consideration, with the remaining fifteen chapters following on November 26. Parliament required that each section of the confession be illustrated with proof-texts—a labor that took the committee until April 1647. After another year of close consideration of the text, the confession was adopted for England by Parliament in June 1648. The Scottish Parliament ratified the confession in 1649.

We also have clear and precise documentation concerning the drafting of several of the major sections of the confession. A smaller sub-committee was named on May 12, 1645, in order to expedite the drafting of individual chapters of the confession: it was composed of Thomas Temple, Joshua Hoyle, Thomas Gataker, Robert Harris, Cornelius Burgess, Edward Reynolds, and Charles Herle.[8] In response to the Assembly's request of July 4 that "the sub-committee for the Confession of Faith . . . make report to the Assembly on Monday morning of what is in their hands concerning . . . the Scriptures," the first chapter of the confession, "Of the Holy Scripture," was presented to the Assembly by Dr. Thomas Temple on Monday, July 7, 1645.[9] Debate on the text of the chapter ran from July 7 through July 18 of 1645.[10]

The minutes of the Assembly offer clear references to the progress of debate on the confession, but only seldom record the actual comments and amendments made by members of the Assembly. On July 8, for example, Edward Reynolds, Charles Herle, and Matthew Newcomen were appointed "to take care of the wording of the Confession of Faith, as it is voted in the assembly, . . . and [after conferring with the Scots Commissioners] to report to the assembly when they think fit there should be any alteration in the words."[11] Debate continued on July 11 and 14 with specific reference to "the necessity of inward illumination for understanding" Scripture. On July 15, the Assembly

7. Ibid., 114.
8. Ibid., 91.
9. Ibid., 109–10.
10. Ibid., 110, 115; cf. Mitchell, *History*, 357–58 and Warfield, *Westminster Assembly*, 87–91, 93 on the problem of identifying the committees.
11. Mitchell and Struthers, *Minutes*, 110.

again debated the clause and inserted the word "saving"—yielding the statement that "we acknowledge the inward illumination of the Spirit of God to be necessary for the saving understanding of such things as are revealed in the Word."[12]

The issue addressed here was that the text of Scripture is plain enough in all doctrines necessary to salvation when rightly read and interpreted, and that the illumination of the Spirit adds no new revelation to that which is objectively given in the written Word, but that spiritual illumination is necessary for the salvific appropriation of the doctrines learned from the written Word by ordinary means. The absence of comment in the minutes of the Assembly does not, however, indicate absence of discussion. The minutes are notoriously sparse, and as the notes and recollections of members like Gillespie and Lightfoot frequently indicate, there was often extensive discussion of even slight variations and differences in phrasing, most of which went unrecorded by the official scribes.[13] Unfortunately, Lightfoot's journal concludes on December 31, 1644, and Gillespie's notes terminate with January 3, 1645. Neither offers information concerning the actual conduct of the debates on the confession.

There are, however, several treatises and sermons by Gillespie written with the Assembly and its teachings in view, one of which does relate directly to the chapter of the confession on Scripture. Gillespie had argued the point that "necessary consequences from the written Word of God do sufficiently and strongly prove the consequent or conclusion, if theoretical, to be a certain divine truth which ought to be believed, and, if practical, to be a necessary duty which we are obliged unto, *jure divino*."[14] William Hethrington, in his memoir of Gillespie, believed that several of the chapters of Gillespie's *Miscellany Questions*, including this particular one, were written out as personal preparation for debate in the Assembly. As evidence for this thesis,

---

12. Ibid., 111, 113; cf. Westminster Confession, 1.6.
13. See George Gillespie, *Notes of Debates and Proceedings of the assembly of divines and other Commissioners at Westminster*, ed. David Meek from unpublished manuscripts, in *The Works of Mr. George Gillespie*, 2 vols. (Edinburgh: Ogle, Oliver, and Boyd, 1846), vol. 2, separate pagination; John Lightfoot, *Journal of the Proceedings of the Assembly of Divines*, in *The Whole Works of the Rev. John Lightfoot, D. D. Master of Catharine Hall, Cambridge*, ed. John Rogers Pitman, 13 vols. (London: J. F. Dove, 1825), 13:1–344.
14. George Gillespie, *A Treatise of Miscellany Questions*, ch. 20, in *Works*, 2:100–103.

Hethrington notes not only the relationship between several sections of the *Miscellany Questions* and the topics of the confession but also the use of other chapters of the document, in edited form, in the treatise on church government, *Aaron's Rod*, completed in 1646 and dedicated to the Assembly as a capstone to the Erastian controversy—which fixes the date of the writing of some of the questions before the conclusion of the Assembly.[15] Hethrington does not, however, take up the point in his *History*; and inasmuch as the text of Gillespie's questions does not indicate either by comment or by way of form that they arose in relation to debates on the floor of the Assembly, the questions related to the topics of the confession offer, at best, collateral testimony to the nature of the issues there addressed—and not direct commentary on the text of the confession.[16]

In the two and a half years intervening between July 1645 and January 1647,[17] moreover, the text had been refined and edited by review committee. The review committee, as constituted on December 8, 1645, consisted of Anthony Tuckney, Edward Reynolds, Matthew Newcomen, and Jeremiah Whitaker, with the addition, on June 17, 1646, of John Arrowsmith.[18] A reference to further debate on Scripture, followed by the initial report on chapter 2 of the confession, is found in the minutes for July 18, and on the following day, the Assembly instructed the committee on review (presumably Tuckney, Reynolds, Newcomen, Whitaker, and Arrowsmith) to take final responsibility for the "wording and methodizing of the Confession of Faith."[19] Subsequent references to debate on the confession do not mention Scripture, but indicate discussion of other topics.[20] Debate resumed on January 7, 1647, with reference to the proof-texts supplied by the committee, and continued through January 15.

15. Hethrington, *Memoir of the Rev. George Gillespie*, in Gillespie, *Works*,1:xxxiv.

16. Hethrington, *History of the Westminster Assembly*, 281–85; cf. Jack B. Rogers, *Scripture in the Westminster Confession: A Problem of Historical Interpretation for American Presbyterianism* (Grand Rapids: Eerdmans, 1967), 333–39.

17. Note that, in the seventeenth century, the English calendar still began its year on Lady Day, March 25—with the result that January 1645 fell six months *after* July 1645 (the preceding January being January 1644), yielding two and a half years between July 1645 and January 1647.

18. Mitchell and Struthers, *Minutes*, 168, 245.

19. Ibid., 245.

20. Ibid., 114–15.

The Theological Context of the Confession and Catechisms

By way of approach to the theology of the Confession and catechisms, it may be important to note the varied opinions of the documents registered by writers in the twentieth century. On the specific topic of Scripture, not only has the meaning of the doctrine expressed in the confession and catechisms been debated, its relationship to the Reformation and to the era of Reformed orthodoxy has been contested. Older scholarship, most notably the work of Warfield, Schaff, and McNeill, presented the confession as standing in continuity with the thought of the Reformers and also as reflecting the orthodoxy and scholasticism of its era.[21] More recently, Rogers accepted the basic outlines of the rather discredited "Calvin against the Calvinists" approach to Reformed orthodoxy, and at the same time has continued to argue the continuity of the teaching of the confession with the theology of the Reformation. In Rogers's view, the British Reformed theology of the confession and its authors did not partake of the scholastic orthodoxy and Christian Aristotelianism of the Continental Reformed thought of the era.[22] A rather different use of the "Calvin against the Calvinists" refrain is characteristic of the claims of T. F. and J. B. Torrance concerning the confession and catechisms: in their view, the confession and the catechisms stand in stark discontinuity with the thought of the Reformers precisely because they belong to the era of orthodoxy.[23] Both of these misreadings of the Westminster Standards represent an ahistorical approach to both Reformation and orthodoxy resting on a larding-over of the documents with heavy theological biases. As the documentation that follows will show, Rogers's

21. Warfield, *Westminster Assembly*, 155–333; Philip Schaff, *The Creeds of Christendom, with a History and Critical Notes*, 6th ed., 3 vols. (New York, 1931; repr. Grand Rapids: Baker Book House, 1983), 1:760–62, 766–68; John T. McNeill, *The History and Character of Calvinism* (New York: Oxford University Press, 1954), 325–26.

22. Rogers, *Scripture in the Westminster Confession*, passim; and Jack B. Rogers and Donald K. McKim, *The Authority and Interpretation of the Bible: An Historical Approach* (San Francisco: Harper and Row, 1979), 200–218.

23. T. F. Torrance, *Scottish Theology: From John Knox to John McLeod Campbell* (Edinburgh: T. & T. Clark, 1996); cf. James B. Torrance, "Calvin and Puritanism in England and Scotland —Some Basic Concepts in the Development of 'Federal Theology,'" in *Calvinus Reformator* (Potchefstroom: Potchefstroom University for Christian Higher Education, 1982), 264–77; idem, "Strengths and Weaknesses of the Westminster Theology," in *The Westminster Confession in the Church Today*, ed. Alisdair Heron (Edinburgh: Saint Andrews Press, 1982), 40–53.

and the Torrances' understandings of the confession and its authors are quite unsupportable.

The identity of the framers of the chapter on Scripture and the content of their writings are certainly significant to the understanding of the document—as is the Reformed theological tradition in which they were trained. The Westminster Confession itself, though not written in a scholastic style and not properly a theological system, could not have been written apart from the intellectual background of Protestant orthodoxy and scholasticism, with its strong components of logic, dialectic, and Aristotelian causality. The framers of the confession, most of whom had been educated at Cambridge, had followed a fairly typical late scholastic curriculum,[24] and had, among other works, read with care Calvin's *Institutes*, which remained standard in theology at Cambridge.[25] They had certainly also read or examined theological works of their own English predecessors and contemporaries, various medieval scholastics, and representative continental theologians of the era. There was, in fact, a consistent and fruitful intellectual commerce between England and the Continent throughout the sixteenth and seventeenth centuries: theologians like Perkins, William Whitaker, Ames, Weemes, Gataker, Twisse, and Owen read widely in the works of Continental theologians and were, themselves, highly regarded on the Continent, especially by the Dutch and Swiss Reformed. Some of this theological "reading list" of mid-seventeenth-century English theologians can be identified in the numerous citations offered in the writings of Edward Leigh, who was a member of Parliament at the time of the Westminster Assembly.[26]

The confession reflects, moreover, the shape of the Reformed orthodox theological system, built upon the two *principia* of Scripture and the triune God, lacking only the prior *locus*, the prolegomenon to theology, in which the basic definition of the subject was set forth. The absence of this first *locus* is easily explained by the fact that this is a

24. See William T. Costello, *The Scholastic Curriculum at Early Seventeenth-Century Cambridge* (Cambridge, MA: Harvard University Press, 1958).
25. See Charles D. Cremeans, *The Reception of Calvinistic Thought in England* (Urbana: University of Illinois Press, 1949).
26. See Edward Leigh, *A Treatise of Divinity* (London, 1646), and idem, *A Systeme or Body of Divinity* (London, 1662).

38

confession and not a system properly so-called. The subjects included in the first two chapters of the confession compare almost exactly with the subjects of the *loci de scriptura* and *de deo* of the scholastic systems. In short, the Westminster Confession is a product of the age of scholastic orthodoxy that draws both in form and in content upon the systematic development of Reformed orthodoxy—but it is also a product that respects the difference in genre between system and confession.[27] The confession intentionally offers no more detail than its authors thought necessary for a basic definition of Reformed doctrine—and many topics found in the theological systems of the day are entirely omitted from consideration.

The Westminster Standards also well illustrate the path of doctrinal exposition taken by Protestant scholasticism and stand in relation to the confessions of the preceding century, much as the theological systems of the era of orthodoxy stand to the more systematic efforts of the Reformers. The two catechisms of the Assembly follow a logical and systematic form based on earlier documents of the orthodox or scholastic era, notably, a series of predecessor catechisms,[28] Ussher's *Body of Divinity*, and, according to some, Wollebius's *Compendium*, which had gone through a series of Latin editions around the time of the Assembly, and which was translated into English shortly afterward.[29] As for the confession, its reliance on the work of Ussher, its intellectual and spiritual kinship to the theological works of various members of the Assembly,[30] and the subsequent elaboration of the

27. Contra Rogers, *Scripture in the Westminster Confession*, and Rogers and McKim, *Authority and Interpretation of the Bible*, both of which attempt to free the confession from "scholastic" influences by dating the beginnings of Reformed scholasticism in England after the time of the confession and by arguing a "Platonic" and therefore nonscholastic philosophy underlying the confession. See the blistering but nonetheless substantive critique in John D. Woodbridge, *Biblical Authority: A Critique of the Rogers/McKim Proposal* (Grand Rapids: Zondervan, 1982); and note the alternative explanation of the issue in Richard A. Muller, *After Calvin: Essays in the Development of a Theological Tradition* (New York: Oxford University Press, 2004), 27; also note Richard A. Muller, *Post-Reformation Reformed Dogmatics*, 4 vols. (Grand Rapids: Baker Book House, 2003), 1-1.1, 1.3, 2.6, 4.1–2, 8.1, 8.3, 2-2.2–3, 7.4(C).

28. See the documents gathered in Alexander Mitchell, *Catechisms of the Second Reformation*, with historical introduction and biographical notes (London: Nisbet, 1886).

29. Johannes Wollebius, *Compendium theologiae* (London, 1642, 1647, 1648, 1654, 1655, 1657, 1661); translated by Alexander Ross as *The Abridgement of Christian Divinity* (London, 1650, 1656, 1660); and cf. the comments of Schaff, *Creeds*, 1:756.

30. E.g., John Arrowsmith, *Armilla Catechetica; A Chain of Principles: Or, an Orderly Concatenation of Theological Aphorisms and Exercitations* (Cambridge, 1659); William Gouge, *A*

Assembly's work into large-scale systems reflective of the patterns of argument of the era of orthodoxy, by writers like Dickson,[31] Vincent,[32] Flavel,[33] Watson,[34] and Ridgley,[35] all point to its place at the center of the development of an English Reformed version of Protestant scholastic theology.

The chapter on Scripture presents a cohesive statement of virtually all points of the doctrine of Scripture found in the Reformed dogmatics of the sixteenth and seventeenth centuries, but developed in a confessional rather than in a fully dogmatic or scholastic form. Leith notes that this first chapter—like all that follow—is remarkably concise and entirely devoid of unnecessary or tendentious argument: we encounter here a simple statement of the contents of the canon of Scripture and no debate on problems of authorship; we read a strong statement of the inspiration and authority of Scripture, but no attempt to formulate a particular theory of inspiration.[36] As with the Irish Articles, Westminster marks a formal development of the Reformed doctrine of Scripture without any abandonment of the basic premises of early Reformed doctrine.

Although written with a retrospective glance at the Thirty-nine Articles, the Westminster Confession most clearly echoes the order

Short Catechisme (London, 1615); Thomas Gataker, *A Short Catechism* (London, 1624); idem, *Shadowes without Substance, or Pretended New Lights . . . Divers Points of Faith and Passages of Scripture . . . Vindicated and Explained* (London, 1646); William Twisse, *A Brief Catecheticall Exposition* (London, 1645); and idem, *The Scriptures Sufficiency* (London, 1656); and note the *English Annotations* (London, 1645): among the authors, John Ley, William Gouge, Francis Taylor, Edward Reynolds, Thomas Gataker, and Daniel Featley were members of the Westminster Assembly.

31. David Dickson, *The Summe of Saving Knowledge* (Edinburgh, 1671); and idem, *Truth's Victory Over Error* (Edinburgh, 1684).

32. Thomas Vincent, *An explicatory catechism, or, An explanation of the Assemblies Shorter catechism* (London: George Calvert et al., 1673).

33. John Flavel, *An Exposition of the Assembly's Catechism, with Practical Inferences from Each Question*, in *The Works of John Flavel*, 6 vols. (1820; repr. Edinburgh: Banner of Truth, 1968), 6:138–317.

34. Thomas Watson, *A Body of Practical Divinity* (London, 1692).

35. Thomas Ridgley, *A Body of Divinity: Wherein the Doctrines of the Christian Religion are Explained and Defended, being the Substance of Several Lectures on the Assembly's Larger Catechism*, 2 vols. (London, 1731–33).

36. Cf. John H. Leith, *Assembly at Westminster: Reformed Theology in the Making* (Richmond, 1973), 75–76.

and contents of the Irish Articles. As Warfield long ago pointed out, the confession so fully stands in the line of the orthodox Reformed theology of the sixteenth and seventeenth centuries, whether that of the English Puritans or that of the Continental writers, that "there is scarcely a leading divine of the first three quarters of a century of Reformed theology, who has written at large on the Scriptures, from whom statements may not be drawn so as to make them appear to be the immediate sources of some of the Westminster sections."[37] As examples of this Reformed theology, Warfield notes John Calvin, John Ball, Gulielmus Bucanus, and then, borrowing at length on Heppe, he cites Amandus Polanus, Ludovicus Crocius, Marcus Friedrich Wendelin, Daniel Chamier, Franz Burman, and Johann Heinrich Heidegger as witnesses to his contention.[38] Indeed, there is little difference in doctrine and perspective between the divines of the Westminster Assembly and their Continental Reformed orthodox counterparts. Specifically, we must repudiate as quite unsupported by the sources any attempt to claim that the Continental Reformed theologians were led by their scholastic method to place reason prior to faith in their understanding of theological *principia*, that "scholasticism" leads theology toward such a conclusion, or that the priority of the faithful reading of Scripture over rational argumentation indicates opposition either to scholasticism or to the use of Aristotelian philosophy.[39]

37. Warfield, *Westminster Assembly*, 161.

38. Ibid.; cf. the comments of John T. McNeill, *History and Character of Calvinism*, 325; contra Rogers, *Scripture in the Westminster Confession*, and Rogers and McKim, *Authority and Interpretation of the Bible*. It is simply a misreading of seventeenth-century intellectual history to claim that the Westminster Confession is not the product of a scholastic training and that the beginnings of Protestant scholasticism in England can be marked in the slightly later work of John Owen: scholastic Protestantism was in full flower in England in the time of Perkins, and the Westminster Confession is one of its contributions to the Reformed tradition: contra Rogers and McKim, *Authority and Interpretation*, 202–3, 218–23.

39. Contra Rogers and McKim, *Authority and Interpretation*, 106, 148, 165, 202–5, where the authors assume, without documentation, that a priority of faith over reason is characteristic of a Platonic approach and then, again without documentation, argue that the continental theologians of the era, as Aristotelians, must have placed reason before faith—as if the relation between faith and reason could be settled by appeal to these broad philosophical perspectives; cf. the far more accurate comments of Schaff in *Creeds*, 1:760: "the Westminster Confession sets forth the Calvinistic system in its scholastic maturity. . . . The confession had the benefit of the Continental theology"; cf. Warfield, *Westminster Assembly*, 159–69; and note the discussion of this issue in Muller, *Post-Reformation Reformed Dogmatics*, 1:8.1(C), 8.3(B), 2:2.1(B.4), 4.2–4.3.

The Westminster Standards represent, therefore, in confessional form, the codification into a rule or norm of faith of the ground gained for English Reformed theology by writers like Fenner, Perkins, Cartwright, Ames, Rollock, and Whitaker, and interpreted in the first half of the seventeenth century by Reynolds, Downame, Ussher, Burgess, Fisher, Featley, Gataker, Gouge, Leigh, and others. Of these thinkers, moreover, Reynolds and Gataker were among the authors of the confession, Featley was a member of the Westminster Assembly until 1648, Ussher (who wrote the Irish Articles) had been invited to serve in the Assembly, and Leigh was a member of Parliament following 1640 and appears to have attended some of the sessions. The confession and the catechisms would also provide the basis of fuller systematic theologies in the form of commentaries or catechetical lectures such as the catechetical systems of Watson, Vincent, Flavel, and Ridgley or the confessional commentary of Dickson.

All the members of the committee for the Confession of Faith were drawn from the clerical side of the Assembly—none of the Lords or commoners who met at Westminster were asked to participate in the actual process of drafting the document. A fair majority of the members of the committee, moreover, were highly respected theologians and authors, although, arguably, two of the most expert exegetes at the Assembly, John Lightfoot and William Greenhill, did not serve on the committee—nor, indeed, were they among the compilers of the *Annotations* commissioned by Parliament.

The Doctrine of Scripture in the Westminster Confession

Records of the Westminster Assembly manifest no great debate over the subject of the first chapter of the proposed confession. Several of the most important predecessors of the confession—both Helvetic Confessions, the Genevan Harmony, and the Irish Articles—as well as many of the major systems of Reformed theology began with a discussion of the source of theology in the Scriptures. The other option, which became increasingly the model for full-scale systems, was to define "theology" and to speak of the knowledge of God in general before moving on to the scriptural revelation.[40] Westminster does, in fact, note this latter order by commenting briefly on natural knowledge of God, indicating its insufficiency, and pointing to the necessity of the Scriptures. According to the confession, there are two sources, an inward and an outward, of this natural knowledge of God, "the light of nature, and the works of creation and providence." These forms of revelation "do so far manifest the goodness, wisdom, and power of God, as to leave men inexcusable; yet they are not sufficient to give that knowledge of God, and of his will, which is necessary to salvation."[41]

The inability of humanity to attain right knowledge and true worship of God through the light of nature led God to "reveal himself and to declare his will unto his Church."[42] It is worth noting here that neither the text of the confession nor the documents of Reformed theology in the sixteenth and seventeenth centuries permit us to distinguish, as one essay has done, between a "two-source theory of revelation" typical of "scholastic theology" and a "personal revelation" theory characteristic of the Reformers and the Westminster Standards.[43] Application of this kind of language to the interpretation of sixteenth- and seventeenth-century documents betrays an unwittingly anachronistic set of assumptions concerning the teaching of

40. E.g., the Gallican (1559) and Belgic (1561) Confessions; and note Johannes Wollebius, *Compendium theologiae christianae*, new ed. (Neukirchen, 1935); William Ames, *Medulla ss. theologiae* (Amsterdam, 1623; London, 1630); also, *The Marrow of Theology*, trans. with intro. by John Dykstra Eusden (Boston: Pilgrim, 1966; repr. Durham, NC: Labyrinth Press, 1984); Lucas Trelcatius, Jr., *Scholastica et methodica locorum communium Institutio* (London, 1604), trans. as *A Briefe Institution of the Commonplaces of Sacred Divinitie* (London, 1610); Amandus Polanus von Polansdorf, *Syntagma theologiae christianae* (Geneva, 1617), and idem, *The Substance of the Christian Religion* (London, 1595).

41. Westminster Confession, 1:1; cf. Larger Catechism, Q.2: "The very light of nature in man, and the works of God, declare plainly that there is a God; but his word and Spirit only do sufficiently and effectually reveal him unto men for their salvation." In the following essay, I have used the text of the Westminster Confession found in Schaff, *Creeds*, 3:600–73; all other confessional documents from the Assembly have been cited from *Westminster Confession of Faith* (Glasgow: Free Presbyterian Publications, 1994), which (despite its title) contains, in addition to the confession, the texts of both catechisms, the original prefatory letters, texts of the relevant churchly and parliamentary ordinances, the *Sum of Saving Knowledge*, the National Covenant, the Solemn League and Covenant, the *Directory for the Public Worship of God*, the *Form of Presbyterial Church Government*, and the *Directory for Worship*.

42. Westminster Confession, 1:1; in Schaff, *Creeds*, 3:600 et seq.

43. So Rogers and McKim, *Authority and Interpretation*, 203.

43

the Reformers and their successors. Whether we look to Calvin, to the theology of representative Puritan and Reformed scholastic theologians, or to the Westminster Confession itself, we find virtually the same basic set of assumptions: there is a divine revelation in the natural order,[44] and there is an innate sense of the divine in every rational human being;[45] because of the fall and sin, however, neither of these resources can provide a valid, much less a saving, knowledge of God.[46] A second source of revelation and, accompanying it, the redemptive and illuminative work of the Spirit as grounded on the saving work of Christ is now necessary—and necessary in written form—in order for human beings to come to faith and to know of God rightly.[47] That second source is the biblical Word of God, of which Christ or God's covenant in Christ is the "foundation" and "scope."[48]

44. In this and the following four notes, I cite in order a) Calvin and other sixteenth-century Reformed theologians; b) representative Westminster divines; c) English Reformed theologians of the seventeenth century who were not members of the Westminster Assembly; and d) continental orthodox or "scholastic" Reformed theologians. Thus, cf. a) John Calvin, *Institutes of the Christian Religion* (1559), ed. John T. McNeill, trans. F. L. Battles, 2 vols. (Philadelphia: Westminster, 1950), 1.5.1–2, 9–10; 6.1; Wolfgang Musculus, *Loci communes sacrae theologiae* (Basel, 1560; 3rd ed., 1573), cap. i; Peter Martyr Vermigli, *The Common Places of Peter Martyr*, trans. Anthony Marten (London, 1583), 1.2.3; b) Anthony Burgess, *Spiritual Refining: or, a Treatise of Grace and Assurance* (London, 1652), 692–94; William Twisse, *The Riches of God's Love* (London, 1653), 188–89; John Arrowsmith, *A Chaine of Principles* (Cambridge, 1659), 86–87; Edmund Calamy, *The Godly Mans Ark* (London, 1672), 90–93; c) Edward Leigh, *A Systeme or Body of Divinity* (London, 1662), 1–2, 10, 145; James Ussher, *A Body of Divinity, or the Sum and Substance of Christian Religion* (London, 1670), 5–6; d) *Synopsis purioris theologiae, disputationibus quinquaginta duabus comprehensa ac conscripta per Johannem Polyandrum, Andream Rivetum, Antonium Walaeum, Antonium Thysiumin* (Leiden, 1625), 1.8; Francis Turretin, *Institutio theologiae elencticae*, 3 vols. (Geneva, 1679–85; new ed., Edinburgh, 1847), 2.1.3–4.

45. Cf. a) Calvin, *Institutes*, 1.3.1–3; Vermigli, *Common Places*, 1.2.3; b) John White, *A Way to the Tree of Life: Discovered in Sundry Directions for the Profitable Reading of the Scriptures* (London, 1647), 13, 25; Arrowsmith, *Chaine of Principles*, 128; William Bridge, *Scripture Light, the Most Sure Light* (London, 1656), 32–33; c) Leigh, *Body of Divinity*, 1–2, 145; Ussher, *Body of Divinity*, 3; d) *Synopsis purioris theologiae*, 1.8; Turretin, *Inst. theol. elencticae*, 2.1.3–4.

46. Cf. a) Calvin, *Institutes*, 1.5.11–15; Vermigli, *Common Places*, 1.2.8; b) Burgess, *Spiritual Refining*, 692–94; c) Leigh, *Body of Divinity*, 146; Ussher, *Body of Divinity*, 6; d) Pierre Du Moulin, *A Treatise of the Knowledge of God* (London, 1634), 24–25, 36; Turretin, *Inst. theol. elencticae*, 1.4.3, 20.

47. Cf. a) Calvin, *Institutes*, 1.5.1–2; Musculus, *Loci communes*, i; Vermigli, *Common Places*, 1.4.15; b) White, *Way to the Tree of Life*, 25, 67–68; Arrowsmith, *Chaine of Principles*, 86–87, 128; Calamy, *Godly Mans Ark*, 90–93; c) Leigh, *Body of Divinity*, 101, 145–46; Ussher, *Body of Divinity*, 6–7; d) *Synopsis purioris theologiae*, 2.6–09; Turretin, *Inst. theol. elencticae*, 2.1–2.

48. Cf. a) Calvin, *Institutes*, 1.6.1–4; Bullinger, *Second Helvetic Confession*, 1.1–5; idem, *Decades*, 1.1.37–38; Musculus, *Loci communes*, xxi; Zacharias Ursinus, *Loci theologici*, in *Opera theologica*, 3 vols. (Heidelberg, 1612), 1, col. 426; b) Edward Reynolds, *An Explication of the*

This juxtaposition of the insufficiency of natural revelation with the sufficiency of Scripture expresses the typical Reformed paradox of the natural knowledge of God: the "light of nature" and the "works of creation and providence" manifest the goodness, wisdom, and power of God enough to leave human beings inexcusable in their sin, but do not provide a revelation of God sufficient to save humanity. There is no denial of natural revelation, nor is there a denial of natural theology in a limited sense, but the noetic effect of sin is such that even Christian doctrines concerning the natural order, like creation and providence, will rest primarily on Scripture for their content. This is one of the themes resident in the *duplex cognitio dei* enunciated by Calvin as one of the formal principles of theology—and it is also an assumption held by Reformed orthodox writers of the seventeenth century.[49] (It is certainly not a point on which one can separate the theology of the Reformers from that of their orthodox successors.) It serves to press Reformed theology away from natural revelation toward the supernatural and, in view of the difficulty of preserving individual unwritten revelations and of the cessation of God's "former ways" of "revealing his will," toward recognition of the necessity of the written Word as contained in the Old and New Testaments.

The confession therefore distinguishes between the direct revelation of God by various means to the faithful in ancient times and the inscripturation of that revelation, in continuity with the Reformed orthodox discussion of a distinction between written and unwritten word (*verbum agraphon* and *verbum engraphon*) that, prior to the writing of Scripture, "It pleased the Lord, at sundry times, and in divers manners, to reveal himself and to declare his will unto his Church."[50] Not only continuing "corruption of the flesh, and the malice of Satan and of the world," but also the cessation of immediate revelations

---

Hundred and Tenth Psalm, wherein the Several Heads of the Christian Religion therein contained .. . are largely explained and applied (1632), in *The Whole Works of the Right Rev. Edward Reynolds*, 6 vols. (London: B. Holdsworth, 1826), 2.5–6; Gillespie, *A Treatise of Miscellany Questions*, ch. 21, in *Works*, 2.105–6; c) Leigh, *Body of Divinity*, fol. C1 recto; 5, 7; d) Du Moulin, *A Treatise of the Knowledge of God*, 56–57; Witsius, *De oeconomia foederum Dei cum hominibus libri quattuor* (Utrecht, 1694), IV.vi.2; Turretin, *Inst. theol. elencticae*, 2.2.1. On the issue of the "scope of scripture," see Muller, *PRRD*, 2.3.5.

49. Cf. Turretin, *Inst. theol. elencticae*, 2.1.5, with the discussion in *PRRD*, 1.6.2–6.3.
50. Westminster Confession, 1.1.

necessitated the careful compilation of God's Word: "for the better preserving and propagating of the truth, and for the more sure establishment of the Church," God committed "the same" special revelation "wholly unto writing." This claim, which can be found in Reformed theological documents from the time of the *Ten Theses of Bern* (1528) to the end of the era of scholastic orthodoxy, makes a significant historical point over against the Roman Catholic claims of a normative unwritten tradition and of the priority of an unwritten Word over the written one. The Protestant rejoinder, echoed in the Westminster Confession, was that, from a historical perspective, it was quite true that an unwritten Word preceded the written Word—but equally so it was quite clear that the written Word had superseded the unwritten, and for very good reason. As Edward Leigh wrote, distinctly echoing the *Ten Theses of Bern*, if we consider "the Word . . . as written and clothed with words, . . . the Church was before Scripture," but if we consider "the matter and sense or meaning, . . . the Scripture was more ancient than the Church, because the Church is gathered and governed by it."[51] And given the presence of the normative, written Word in the Scriptures, the Westminster Confession can conclude that "those former ways of God's revealing his will unto his people [are] now ceased."[52]

Scripture, thus otherwise identified as "the Word of God written," consists of the books of the Old and New Testaments. The confession enumerates the books and then states, with no further elaboration, "All of which are given by inspiration of God, to be the rule of faith and life."[53] The confession does not, as has often been noted, define a particular theory of inspiration. This is the case, at least in part, because of the various understandings of the relationship between the work of the Holy Spirit and the efforts of the human writers of Scripture present in the works of Puritan and Reformed orthodox writers of the era.[54] The lack of definition is certainly also due to the genre of the document. A confession, by nature, is not as detailed as a dogmatic

51. Leigh, *Body of Divinity*, 1.2 (24).
52. Westminster Confession, 1.1; cf. the discussion in Muller, *PRRD*, 2.3.3–4.
53. Westminster Confession, 1.1–2; cf. Larger Catechism, Q.3: "The holy scriptures of the Old and New Testaments are the word of God, the only rule of faith and obedience."
54. See Muller, *PRRD*, 2.4.2.

treatise and, by intention, does not demand confessional commitment to the niceties of theological system. Nonetheless, examination of the writings of various Westminster divines evidences continuity between their formulations of the doctrine of inspiration and the formulations offered by continental theologians of the seventeenth century. John White held that "the holy Ghost not only suggested to [the Pen-men of those sacred writings] the substance of the doctrine which they were to deliver . . . but besides hee supplied to them the very phrases, method, and whole order of those things that are written in the Scriptures." Yet, in so inspiring the very words of the text, the Spirit in no way "altered the phrase and manner of speaking, wherewith custom and education had acquainted those that wrote the Scriptures" but rather "drew their naturall style to an higher pitch, in divine expressions, fitted to the subject in hand."[55] White explicitly compares the rougher style of Amos and James with the more elegant and learned styles of Isaiah and Paul.[56] Typical of this view of inspiration is its juxtaposition of "words" with "substance"—*verba* with *res*—for the sake of arguing verbal inspiration of the text in the original languages but also at the same time stressing the importance of the things signified by the words, namely the doctrines conveyed by the text. As David Dickson (echoing the Shorter Catechism) would comment on the Westminster Confession, ca. 1650, "Scripture" or "Word" indicates not so much "the bare letters or the several words" as "the Doctrine or Will of God," the teaching found in the text.[57]

The apocryphal books are to be excluded from this characterization since they are not "of divine inspiration . . . and therefore as of no authority in the Church of God."[58] Westminster enumerates the books in the canon but—in contrast to earlier post-Tridentine Reformed

55. White, *A Way to the Tree of Life*, 60–62; cf. *Synopsis purioris theologiae*, 3.7; Pictet, *Theol. chr.*, 1.7.2; Mastricht, *Theoretico-practica theologia*, 1.2.12; Witsius, *De prophetis et prophetia*, in *Miscellanea sacra libri IV* (Utrecht, 1692), 1.3.3;4.1; and note the discussion in Muller, *PRRD*, 2.4.2(B).

56. White, *A Way to the Tree of Life*, 62.

57. Dickson, *Truth's Victory Over Error*, 6; cf. Shorter Catechism, Q.2: "The word of God, which is contained in the scriptures of the Old and New Testaments, is the only rule to direct us how we may glorify and enjoy [God]"; and see also Burman, *Synopsis theologiae*, 1.3.2; Leigh, *Body of Divinity*, 1.2 (p. 7); Turretin, *Inst. theol. elencticae*, 2.2.4: and note the discussion in Muller, *PRRD*, 2:3.3–4.

58. Westminster Confession, 1.3.

confessions—does not list the Apocrypha by name.[59] The identification of the canonical books as "the Word of God written" maintains
the larger sense of "Word of God" found in the earlier confessions, as
does the concluding statement of the confession that "the Supreme
Judge of all controversies" in religion is "the Holy Spirit speaking in
Scripture."[60] The canon and the text of the canon is genuinely Word,
but it is also true that Word (in its prior sense as the Logos of God)
and Spirit work through Scripture.

Clearly drawing upon the debate between Protestant and Roman
theologians over the role of the church in determining the authority of
Scripture, in language reflecting nearly all of the orthodox Reformed
theological systems, Westminster asserts:

> The authority of the Holy Scripture, for which it ought to be believed
> and obeyed, dependeth not upon the testimony of any man or church,
> but wholly upon God (who is truth itself), the Author thereof; and
> therefore it is to be received, because it is the Word of God.[61]

The authority of Scripture rests not on human testimony but on divine authorship.[62] The confession also balances its categorical statement of biblical authority with a series of collateral testimonies to the
divinity of the text—in all of which, however, the word "authority" is
lacking. In discussing how Scripture ought to be read and interpreted,
the confession similarly balances outward testimony, objective marks
of divinity, and the external exegetical analysis of text with the inward
assurance of authority and inward illumination of the heart provided
by the Holy Spirit.

Thus, even though the authority of Scripture in no way depends
"upon the testimony of any man or church," people are surely "moved
and induced" to "an high and reverent esteem of the holy Scripture"
by the church.[63] The confessional point reflects distantly the Reformation debate over Augustine's statement that, had it not been for

59. Cf., e.g., Irish Articles, 3.
60. Westminster Confession, 1.2–3, 10.
61. Ibid., 1.4; cf. Turretin, *Inst. theol. elencticae*, 2.4.1.
62. Westminster Confession, 1.4.
63. Ibid, 1.5.

the church, he would not have believed the gospel. To the Roman claim that Augustine, so often favorably cited by the Reformers, had acknowledged the authority of the church as prior to and necessary to the establishment of the authority of Scripture, Protestant theologians had replied that Augustine had certainly been moved to study Scripture by the church—and that this alone was the sense of his comment.[64] The church had directed Augustine toward Scripture, but the Scripture itself had demonstrated its authority to him. The point is important to the catholicity of the Reformation and, by extension, of the Westminster Confession. By affirming the authority of Scripture as resting on its identification as the Word of the divine Author, while at the same time recognizing ecclesial location and recommendation of the text, the Westminster divines had in fact asserted the connection between their confession and the church of all ages.

Persuasion of the divinity of Scripture, like persuasion of its authority, looks finally to God alone—but it is the case that some outward testimony or evidence must also be objectively present. Once again we are in the company of Calvin, but also of later English and Continental Reformed writers. None of these thinkers—certainly none of the scholastic orthodox writers—ever thought to rest the authority of the text on empirical evidence of divine workmanship, but they nonetheless thought it important to state the objective marks of the divinity of the text.[65] Given the divine authorship of Scripture—on an analogy with the divine authorship of the world—marks of the Author or Craftsman will be objectively present in his work. Thus, the divine authorship of the entirety of Scripture necessarily leads to "the consent of all the parts," inasmuch as a single author (particularly an omniscient one!) will not disagree with himself. So too, "the scope" or focus "of the whole" of Scripture is "to give glory to God"— inasmuch as the whole is the revelation of God, authored by God himself. On the same ground, the substance or "matter" of the text

64. Cf. Musculus, *Loci communes*, 21 (*Commonplaces*, 365–67); Calvin, *Institutes*, 1.7.3; Leigh, *Treatise*, 1.2(28), with the discussion in Muller, *PRRD*, 2.5.5(A–B).
65. Cf. Calvin, *Institutes*, 1.8.1–13; Johannes Maccovius, *Loci communes theologici* (Amsterdam, 1658), 2(25–26); Turretin, *Inst. theol. elencticae*, 2.6.6–7, 13; Johann Heinrich Heidegger, *Corpus theologiae* (Zurich, 1700), 2.12–15; with the discussion in Muller, *PRRD*, 2.4.3(C).

49

exhibits a "heavenly" character and the doctrines propounded by this heavenly Word will have a saving "efficacy."[66] Similarly, people are moved to the acceptance of Scripture as authoritative by "the majesty of style," and other marks of divinity found in Scripture, while their "full persuasion" comes only by the inward testimony of the Spirit.[67]

As with the revelation imbedded in the created order, these signs of the divine can never be sufficient ground for belief or for salvation; the fallen human heart must be touched in its subjectivity by the Holy Spirit even for it to understand the objective marks of God's work. Thus, after indicating that the church testifies to the great value of the Scriptures, while the style and contents, the scope and consistency, together with the obvious perfection of the Bible testify to its divine origin, the confession declares:

> Yet, notwithstanding, our full persuasion and assurance of the infallible truth, and divine authority thereof, is from the inward work of the Holy Spirit, bearing witness by and with the Word in our hearts.[68]

Significant, here, is the reversal of the point made by the Irish Articles, namely, "we acknowledge [Scripture] to be given by the inspiration of God, and in that regard to be of most certain credit and highest authority."[69] The authority of Scripture is not grounded by Westminster on the concept of inspiration, but rather on its nature as the Word of the divine Author. The Westminster Standards, thus, contradict Heppe's thesis that orthodoxy moved away from

---

66. Westminster Confession, 1.5.

67. Ibid.; cf. Larger Catechism, Q.4: "The scriptures manifest themselves to be the word of God, by their majesty and purity; by the consent of the parts, and the scope of the whole, which is to give all glory to God; by their light and power to convince and convert sinners, to comfort and build up believers unto salvation: but the Spirit of God bearing witness by and with the scriptures in the heart of man, is alone able fully to persuade it that they are the very word of God."

68. Westminster Confession, 1.5; cf. Larger Catechism, Q.155: "The Spirit of God maketh the reading, but especially the preaching of the word, an effectual means of enlightening, convincing, and humbling sinners; of drawing them out of themselves, and drawing them unto Christ. . . ."

69. Irish Articles, 2, ad fin.

the Reformation stress on Word toward a view of biblical authority grounded on the doctrine of inspiration—as if Word, authority,
and inspiration were concepts that could easily be separated in the
seventeenth-century mind.[70] The confession also maintains the Reformers' emphasis on the internal testimony of the Spirit over the
external or empirical evidences of the divinity of Scripture. In fact,
this patterning of the argument was normative not only for Reformers like Calvin and Bullinger, but also for the orthodox or scholastic
Reformed theologians of the seventeenth century: authority is not
so much a conclusion to be drawn from inspiration as an immediate
corollary of inspiration. "Authority," after all, rests on the identity of
the "author," and in the case of Scripture, inspiration is the manner
in which the Author works. The so-called "evidences of divinity" are
necessary results of the divine working capable of being perceived
by the faithful, not empirical grounds for belief.[71]

Having made the basic point concerning the divinity and authority of the canonical Scriptures, the Westminster Confession moves
on to address the content and the interpretation of the Bible. The
sufficiency and fullness of the biblical revelation for the salvation
of the world is stated and qualified with more precision and clarity
than can be found in any earlier Reformed confession: "The whole
counsel of God, concerning all things necessary for his own glory,
man's salvation, faith and life, is either expressly set down in Scripture, or by good and necessary consequence may be deduced from
Scripture: unto which nothing at any time is to be added, whether
by new revelations of the Spirit, or traditions of men."[72] The biblical
revelation, therefore, is sufficient to the task of saving the human race,
but is also limited in scope.

The infallible truth of a verbally inspired text—which it was certainly the intention of the Westminster Confession to argue—is not
to be confused with the infinite truth of God himself. Here too we

70. Cf. Heinrich Heppe, *Reformed Dogmatics Set Out and Illustrated from the Sources*, rev.
and ed. Ernst Bizer, trans. G. T. Thomson (1950; repr. Grand Rapids: Baker, 1978), 16–17.
71. Cf. Muller, *PRRD*, 2:4.3(B–C).
72. Westminster Confession, 1.6; more simply in the Larger Catechism, Q.5: "The scriptures principally teach, what man is to believe concerning God, and what duty God requires
of man"; cf. Shorter Catechism, Q.3.

encounter a reflection of the Reformed scholastic theological system, specifically of its modest assumptions concerning Scripture and theology.Whereas God's own truth is surely infinite, the truth presented by Scripture, albeit infallibly given, is by nature and necessity finite or "ectypal." If Scripture is not *infinite*, it is nonetheless *sufficient* or entirely perfect to the accomplishment of its purpose. Here again, the confession is in full dialogue with the theology of Reformed orthodoxy: Scripture does not contain knowledge of all things, but only of "all things necessary" for the glory of God "and man's salvation"—indeed, Scripture provides a "full discovery . . . of the only way of man's salvation."[73] In precise parallel with the words of the confession, Edward Leigh could declare, "The holy Scripture doth sufficiently contain and deliver all doctrines which are necessary to us for eternal salvation, both in respect of Faith and good works."[74] There are, therefore, various "circumstances," including some "concerning the worship of God and the government of the church," that are not explicitly defined in Scripture. These are "to be ordered by the light of nature and Christian prudence." And whereas "the general rules of the Word . . . are always to be observed," we must not expect Scripture to offer explicit information about all things—not even all religious things.[75] The doctrine of Scripture is thus safeguarded from a wooden rationalism, and in the life of the church, the realm of *adiaphora* is carefully marked out and preserved from a rigoristic biblicism.

The Westminster Confession, very much like the theology of the Reformers and of the Reformed orthodox, therefore, leaves a good deal of room for the use of reason and the examination of both nature and history. It also assumes, very much in accord with the Reformed theology of the seventeenth century, that the Scripture does not—and need not—provide exhaustive information about the ancient world in general or even about the events that it describes in its own narrative. It is important to recognize, moreover, that these limitations do not stand in tension with or militate against the old Protestant doctrine of verbal inspiration, but in fact belong part and parcel to it: the Holy Spirit used the words, the thought patterns, and the training of a host

---

73. Westminster Confession, 1.6.
74. Leigh, *Treatise*, 1.8(141); cf. Mastricht, *Theoretico-practica theologia*, 1.2.19.
75. Westminster Confession, 1.6.

of diverse human beings in the production of the biblical text. The biblical writers were, to be sure, preserved from their own fallibility, but their heads were not filled with extraneous information.[76] The confession also qualifies its doctrine of the sufficiency and fullness of Scripture with the traditional caveat that not all places in Scripture are clear and plain in their meaning.[77] Nonetheless, it continues, all things "necessary to be known, believed, and observed for salvation" are stated clearly if not in one place in Scripture then in another, and are stated so clearly that "not only the learned, but the unlearned, in a due use of ordinary means, may attain unto a sufficient understanding of them."[78] This relationship between the clarity, sufficiency, and fullness of Scripture, and the right of laity to own and read translations of the Bible, is central to the orthodox Protestant doctrine of Scripture. The declaration of clarity and sufficiency is in fact a declaration of the openness of Scripture to Christians generally set against the Roman Catholic reservation of interpretation to the church hierarchy. "Due use of ordinary means" points to the fact that saving doctrine is available to all—even when the niceties of Hebrew and Greek syntax in a particularly difficult passage may be understood by only a few scholars, a point that, incidentally, justifies and even recommends the use of annotations, linking the theology of the confession to the other major theological project recommended by Parliament.

In other words, this section of the confession points toward a churchly dialogue between exegesis and dogmatic formulation, biblical interpretation and catechesis, homiletics and systematic theology that was presumed necessary, by the seventeenth-century Reformed, for a healthy community of belief, but that is quite without parallel in our own times. Just as it is quite a simple matter to draw parallels between the theology of the Westminster Confession and that of the

76. Cf. Muller, *PRRD*, 2:4.3(B.2–3).
77. Westminster Confession, 1.6.
78. Ibid., 1.7; Larger Catechism, Q.156: "Although all are not to be permitted to read the word publickly to the congregation, yet all sorts of people are bound to read it apart by themselves, and with their families; to which end, the holy scriptures are to be translated out of the original into the vulgar languages"; *Directory for Family Worship*, 419: "in every family where there is any that can read, the holy scriptures should be read ordinarily to the family"; cf. Leigh, *Treatise*, 1.8(140–41).

large-scale dogmatic systems of the era, it is also quite easy to move from the confession to the homiletical literature of the day and find close parallels—or from the homiletical literature to various commentaries and then back to the theological systems. Whereas, in other words, there are clearly various levels of difficulty in the theological expression of the day, there is no point in the spectrum of statement at which there is disjunction between lay piety and professional theology or between biblical exegesis and theological formulation.[79]

In following the Reformers and the Reformed orthodox in setting aside the churchly hierarchy and, indeed, the tradition as norms for the interpretation of Scripture, the Westminster Confession declares that Scripture itself is the guide to its own interpretation. This point is implied in the declaration that Scripture is the ultimate norm of doctrine, but it had not been stated explicitly in any of the great Reformed confessions prior to Westminster. Here, the hermeneutical principle of the *analogia Scripturae*, previously developed only in theological systems, attains confessional status. Scripture is the infallible rule of faith and life—and "the infallible rule of interpretation of Scripture is the Scripture itself."[80] The difficult passages must be explained by comparison with the clearer passages; and the body of Christian doctrine must be filled out by a process of drawing interpretive conclusions from the text. The point of the confession is not, however, that all texts in Scripture can be understood easily once the proper comparison has been made, but only that the basic truths of Christianity are readily available either directly or by inference, and that the overarching scope and purpose of Scripture as a whole provide the best and surest guide to the understanding of particular passages that are unclear in themselves. Many texts will remain obscure—but Christians need not worry that these obscurities will jeopardize their salvation. This pattern for interpretation can be justified, moreover, by the fact that Scripture, governed as it is by "the whole counsel of God," has a single fundamental meaning: its "full sense . . . is not manifold but one."[81] Nonetheless, the mere address of reason to the

---

79. See Muller, *PRRD*, 2:7.5(B).
80. Westminster Confession, 1.9.
81. Ibid., cf. 1.6 with 9; thus also, the Larger Catechism, Q.4 can speak of "the scope of the whole [of scripture], which is to give all glory to God."

text does not produce salvation; and there are some issues in the life of the church not directly addressed by Scripture. The confession assumes that a "saving understanding" of the Word, as distinct from a historical and rational understanding, rests on the inward illumination of the Spirit.[82]

Even so, in Gillespie's discussion of the normative character of necessary consequences drawn from the text, there is neither a recourse to unredeemed reason as a standard of authority nor an assumption that a normative truth in theology can arise somehow outside of Scripture by a process of deduction. Gillespie denies specifically that the reason used to draw the conclusion "can be the ground of our belief or conscience." The ground for belief is not the rational process, but the self-evidencing truth of the conclusion itself—and the conclusion, by implication, is not a creation of the mind of the reasoner, but is lodged in the language of the test itself, as discerned by reason. Gillespie argues, moreover, that "natural reason arguing in divine things from natural and carnal principles" cannot draw the proper conclusions, but only "reason captivated and subdued to the obedience of Christ."[83] His point parallels that made in the confession and by other theologians concerning the necessity of the illumination of the Spirit in the interpretation of Scripture and in the recognition of its authority.

It is important to note here that the Westminster Confession rests on what is often called a precritical hermeneutic. It shares, in other words, with the Reformers, and to a certain extent with the patristic and medieval exegetes, a perspective on the text and meaning of Scripture that separates it from the assumptions of modern historical-critical exegesis. Its doctrine of inspiration, parallel to the teaching of contemporary English and Continental Reformed thinkers, and in accord with the views of the Reformers, attributed primary authorship to God and a

82. Westminster Confession, 1.6.

83. Gillespie, *Miscellany Questions*, 101; cf. Dickson, *Truth's Victory Over Error*, 12–13; Gataker, *Shadowes without Substance*, 82; note also that the point is made by Zanchi, *Praefatiuncula in locos communes*, in *Operum theologicorum*, 8 vols. (Geneva, 1617), vol. 8, cols. 417–18; William Whitaker, *A Disputation on Holy Scripture, against the Papists, especially Bellarmine and Stapleton*, trans. and ed. William Fitzgerald (Cambridge: Cambridge University Press, 1849), 9.5(470–71); Leonhard Riissen, *Summa theologiae didactico-elencticae* (1695; Frankfurt and Leipzig, 1731), 2.12, 17.

secondary, instrumental authorship to the human writers of the text. This double attribution of authorship allowed the Westminster divines and their contemporaries to explain the variety of style, viewpoint, and even the limited perspective of the biblical writers, and at the same time to assume that the ultimate meaning of the text, as given by the divine Author, was never to be exhausted by the original historical context of a biblical book or, indeed, of a pericope in the text.[84] Meaning was, of course, to be located in the literal sense of the words of the text, but the literal sense itself, given the ultimate Author of Scripture, receives its significance from the scope and reference of the text in relation to the whole of the canon.

Thus, if the Westminster Confession argues the necessity of translation and the propriety of the use of Scripture by the unlearned, it also insists upon the priority of the Hebrew and Greek originals of the books of the Bible, and ultimately lodges all authority in the text as preserved in the ancient languages. The Hebrew and Greek texts are the "authentic" Scriptures that were "immediately inspired by God, and by his singular care and providence kept pure in all ages."[85] "Final appeal" in all religious controversy, therefore, must be to the text in the original languages rather than to translations. The detail, here, is once again greater than that of previous confessions, but it cannot be claimed that we have entered the realm of dogmatic system. There is no elaboration of discussion distinguishing between "Words" (*verba*) and "substance" (*res*) such as appears in the systems of the day—although the confession does consistently refer to the "matter," i.e., the meaning or substance of the text that lies behind the words. There is also no discussion of the *autographa*, even in the seventeenth-century form of the argument, which simply argued for the priority of Hebrew and Greek as the languages of the original "autograph" copies, without any attempt to enlist these no-longer-existent texts for doctrinal argument. The emphasis of the confession, however, parallels this more detailed systematic argument

84. Cf. David C. Steinmetz, "The Superiority of Precritical Exegesis," in *A Guide to Contemporary Hermeneutics: Major Trends in Biblical Interpretation*, ed. Donald K. McKim (Grand Rapids: Eerdmans, 1986), 65–77, with idem, "Theology and Exegesis: Ten Theses," in ibid., 27; and on seventeenth-century exegetical theory and practice, see Muller, *PRRD*, 2:7.3–4.

85. Westminster Confession, 1.8.

by stressing the prior authority of the original-language texts currently known to the church.[86]

"The Holy Spirit speaking in Scripture" stands as the "Supreme Judge" of "all controversies of religion."[87] In this final statement, which subordinates "all decrees of councils, opinions of ancient writers, doctrines of men, and private spirits" to the scriptural rule, the confession comes full circle in its discussion of authority and reflects on its earlier distinction between the outward, objective divinity of the text and the inward persuasion of the Spirit. The "sacred page" itself, brought forward in its objectivity, is the final rule of faith and practice, but only in the context of faithful listening to the Holy Spirit speaking. The point also relates to the assumption of the inspiration of Scripture: the Holy Spirit speaks in the words of the text because the words of the text, albeit from the vocabulary and reflective of the thought-world of its human authors, are also the words chosen by God to be his Word. Or, similarly, this final point concerning the Spirit speaking in Scripture can also be connected directly with the older patterns of biblical interpretation indicated by the confession: the difficult passages are to be elucidated by the clearer passages because the "true and full sense of any Scripture" can and ought to be searched out in other texts throughout the canon, and because the text speaks in a single rather than in a manifold way. The point, in brief, is that the meaning of the text is lodged in the canonical whole in its ongoing address to the church. This is not a dead text demanding archaeological examination, but a living text in and through which its primary Author, God, speaks by the Spirit. Once again, the confession echoes both the theology and the hermeneutics of the day.

Concluding Reflections

In sum, the doctrine of Scripture presented in the Westminster Standards reflects both the tradition of Reformed theology, with its roots in the Reformers' use of earlier conceptions of the priority of the biblical norm over secondary traditionary norms, in the developing

86. Cf. the discussion in Muller, *PRRD*, 2:6.2(A).
87. Westminster Confession, 1.10.

trajectory of philological understanding of the text and of emphasis on the literal sense as the foundation of meaning, and the assumption (also found in both late medieval and Reformation-era theology) that the text of Scripture provided principial or axiomatic truths from which right conclusions could be drawn for the sake of the formulation of Christian teaching. These basic assumptions of the confession evidence its continuity with the Reformation understanding of Scripture, and also with the far more detailed discussion of the doctrine, authority, and interpretation of the Bible found in the thought of the seventeenth-century Reformed orthodox, whether in Britain or on the Continent. The attempt of a writer like Rogers to sever the confession from its scholastic and orthodox intellectual context falls as far short of the mark as the opposite line of argument found in writers like T. F. Torrance, to sever the ties between the confession and the Reformation in order to travesty both the theology of the Westminster Standards and the thought of the Reformed orthodox.

We can also note that the confession's echoes of the theology of the seventeenth century register the distinction of genres of theological exposition characteristic of the era. The confession consistently stands in dialogue and positive relation with both the exegesis and the dogmatics of its day; but just as it does not reproduce the detail of exegetical works, so does it refrain from reproducing the detail of theological systems. It was written by clergy, exegetes, and theologians who had mastered the scholastic method during their university training, but who knew the place of the method and did not use it overtly in their confessional writings. The scholastic or disputative background of the confession is evidenced only by its clarity of definition and formulation and, when comparison is made, by the congruence of its teaching with the more elaborate argument of the dogmatic treatises and systems of the time. This congruence is also evident when comparison is made with commentaries on Scripture written around the time of the confession. The Westminster Confession, in other words, superbly served the church of its time, it continues to bear witness to the achievements in theological definition and formulation characteristic of the era of orthodoxy, and it offers a model confessional synthesis of churchly theological and exegetical practices. It is to this latter issue that we turn in the following essay.

4

"Either Expressely Set Down . . . or by Good and Necessary Consequence": Exegesis and Formulation in the *Annotations* and the Confession

Introduction

In order to examine the relationship of the confessional standards to the exegesis of the sixteenth and seventeenth centuries, my initial intention is to look at three doctrines that are closely related in the standards—namely the divine decrees, providence, and the covenant of works or covenant of life—and then to look primarily to the first edition of the *Annotations*, given that it was available at the time of the drafting of the confession. For the purpose of the present chapter, however, I will look only at two articles of the chapter on the divine decrees and at the chapter on the covenant of works. Other commentaries as well as other writings of the annotators, the framers of the confession, and their contemporaries will also be examined in order to position the *Annotations* and the standards in relation to the Reformed exegetical tradition.

As will be seen in the course of the essay, there is no simple one-to-one correspondence between the *Annotations* and the Westminster Standards—nor ought one to expect such inasmuch as there was no one-to-one correspondence between the annotators and the framers of the confession, and inasmuch as all of these writers, whether annotators or framers, participated in a rather variegated theological and exegetical tradition. There is also the datum that various of the divines of the era, notably Cornelius Burgess, had made the point rather firmly that these were not the Westminster Assembly's own annotations and had never been presented to the Assembly for approval, a point reiterated by the younger Calamy.[1] The *English Annotations* did not have a normative status for the church in England, and they were not an interpretive resource determinative of the meaning of the Westminster Standards. Nonetheless, they provide a highly proximate interpretive benchmark to which the confessional definitions and their proofs can be indexed and compared.

The Divine Decrees—Confessional Formulation and Exegetical Foundations

The third chapter of the Westminster Confession, the definition of "Gods Eternall Decree," offers a highly compressed and exceedingly carefully tooled definition of the Reformed doctrine of predestination, supported by a goodly roster of biblical proofs. The first three sections of the chapter, which contain the basic definition of the decree and of double predestination, in some fourteen lines of text, offer seven marginal notes containing no less than nineteen biblical references. The sixth section, which concerns election, in ten lines of text, provides five marginal notes in which sixteen biblical texts are cited. As is the case with nearly any other sections of the confession, this pattern of citation represents a rather concentrated referencing of Scripture, such that, were the texts written out in full, the confession would have been expanded vastly in its length. For the sake of illustration, I offer the text of the confession with the citations included in brackets:

I. God from all eternity did, by the most wise and holy Counsell of his own Will, freely, and unchangeably ordaine whatsoever comes

---

1. Cornelius Burgess, *No Sacrilege nor Sin to purchase Bishops Lands,* 2d ed. (London: J. C., 1659) cap. iv (87–88); cf. Edmund Calamy the Younger, *Nonconformist Memorial,* 2nd ed. (London, 1677), 1:346.

to passe [a: Eph. 1:11; Rom. 11:33; Heb. 6:17; Rom. 9:15, 18]; yet so as thereby neither is God the Author of sin [b: James 1:13, 17; 1 John 1:5], nor is violence offered to the will of the Creatures, nor is the Liberty or contigencie of second Causes taken away, but rather established [c: Acts 2:23; Matt. 17:12; Acts 4:27, 28; Job 19:11; Prov. 16:33].

II. Although God knows whatsoever may, or can come to passe upon all supposed conditions [d: Acts 15:18; 1 Sam. 23:11–12; Matt. 11:21, 23], yet hath he not decreed anything because he foresaw it as future, or as that which would come to passe upon such conditions [e: Rom. 9: 11, 13, 16, 18].

III. By the Decree of God, for the manifestation of his Glory, some men and Angels [f: 1 Tim. 5:21; Matt. 25:41] are predestinated unto everlasting life, and others fore-ordained to everlasting death [g: Rom. 9:22–23; Eph. 1:5–6; Prov. 16:4].

VI. As God hath appointed the Elect unto glory; so hath he, by the eternall and most free purpose of his Will, fore-ordained all the meanes thereunto [m: 1 Pet. 1:2; Eph. 1:4–5; 2:10; 2 Thess. 2:13]. Wherefore they who are elected, being fallen in Adam, are redeemed by Christ [n: 1 Thess. 5:9–10; Tit. 2:14], are effectually called unto faith in Christ, by his Spirit working in due season, are justified, adopted, sanctified [o: Rom. 8:30; 2 Thess. 2:13], and kept by his power by faith unto salvation [p: 1 Pet. 1:5]. Neither are any other redeemed by Christ, effectually called, justified, adopted, sanctified and saved; but the Elect only [q: John 17:9; Rom. 8:28–39; John 6:64–65; 10:26; 8:47; 1 John 2:19].

With the exception of citations from Proverbs, Job, and 1 Samuel, all citations are drawn from the New Testament, the larger number from the Pauline epistles; but a goodly sampling are taken from the gospel and first epistle of John. There are two each from the gospel of Matthew and the Acts, and a single citation from James. This selection is a matter of interest, given the numerous references to the divine counsel and decree in the Old Testament, notably in the Psalter and in Isaiah—neither of which books is represented in the citations. Still, among the texts that are cited, we do find the primary "seats" or "places" of the doctrine, notably Romans 8–9 and Ephesians 1.

In the case of the third article of the chapter, the referencing of 1 Timothy 5:21 and Matthew 25:41 is most probably intended to demonstrate the confessional point concerning elect (and nonelect) angels, given that the sole reference to human beings in these texts is the inference from the phrase "depart from me, ye cursed" in Matthew 25:41—indicating the damnation of those who denied Christ by ignoring or persecuting his "brethren," and undergirding not so much the confessional pronouncement concerning the predestination of both men and angels as the next confessional phrase, namely that this predestination is of some to everlasting death. In any case, Ley's 1645 annotations make no elaboration on either text—while the 1557 annotations elaborate considerably on the implications of Matthew 25:41 for salvation and damnation, including the comment that damnation is a removal from the presence of God, not in the absolute sense, given divine omnipresence, but in the sense of being deprived of God's "blessed presence."[2]

The remaining phrase of the third article teaches a double decree of predestination and, not surprisingly, cites Romans 9:22–23—the "vessels of wrath fitted for destruction" and the "vessels of mercy afore prepared unto glory." The effect is to offer a single initial proof in which a double decree is clearly identified, and to follow this with two texts, one tracing a predestination to glory, the other implying a foreordination to condemnation: Ephesians 1:5–6, which speaks of foreordination to adoption in Christ; and Proverbs 16:4, where we read that "the Lord hath made all things for himself: yea, even the wicked for the day of evil."

The *English Annotations* here clearly offer exegetical foundation for the confessional statements. Featley's annotation on Romans 9:22 is brief: he refers the reader to his comments on the phrase "one vessel unto honour, and another unto dishonour" in verse 21, where he notes that "out of this corrupt masse [of mankind], it is in Gods power of his free will to appoint some to everlasting glory, and others to ever-

2. *English Annotations* (1645), Matt. 25:41 and 1 Tim. 5:21, in loc.; cf. *English Annotations* (1657), noting that there is no change in the annotation on 1 Tim. 5:21.

lasting shame and ignominie"—an infralapsarian, but double reading on the decree.[3] At Ephesians 1:5–6, Featley also points toward the confessional Reformed position in his exposition of the passage.[4] At Proverbs 16:4, the annotation by Francis Taylor glosses "Lord hath made all things for himself" with the comment "for his own glory"and the following phrase, "yea, even the wicked for the day of evil," with the explanation, "He bringeth wicked men daily into the world, in whose condemnation he intends to glorifie his justice. . . ."

Whereas the *English Annotations* on Proverbs 16:4 are quite brief, Diodati was expansive and explicit, linking the text closely to the usage taken up by the editors of the confession, and even conferring it interpretively with Romans 9:22–23, among other texts:

> *The wicked*] God is not, nor cannot be author or cause of any wickedness in his Creature; and therefore this [text] ought to be understood thus: That all mankind having been corrupted in *Adam*, God nevertheless doth preserve and cause it to fructifie, to draw and save out of them the number of the elect, leaving the reprobate in their originall depravation; by which, and by the wicked acts they derive from thence, he doth condemn them to just punishment to the glory of his justice, Rom. 9:22 and 23; 1 Pet. 2:8; Jude 4.[5]

Taken as a group, as interpreted and even juxtaposed in the exegetical tradition itself, the three texts allow the conclusion that the eternal purpose indicated with reference to the vessels of mercy and wrath is shown to be worked out in the temporal economy in the adoption of some in Christ and in the preparation of others for the "day of evil."

The sixth article of this chapter of the confession takes up election and the doctrine of election and the order of salvation. The first statement of the article runs, "As God hath appointed the Elect unto glory; so hath he, by the eternall and most free purpose of his Will, fore-ordained all the meanes thereunto," with an initial citation of 1 Peter 1:2, "Elect according to the foreknowledge of God the Father,

---

3. *English Annotations* (1645), Rom. 9:22–23, in loc.
4. Ibid., Eph. 1:5–6, in loc.
5. Diodati, *Pious and Learned Annotations*, Prov. 16:4, in loc.

through sanctification of the Spirit, unto obedience and sprinkling of the blood of Jesus Christ." Given the straightforward sense of the text that Peter's salutation identifies election as occurring "through sanctification," "obedience," and the "sprinkling of the blood of Jesus Christ," the confessional interest in declaring that election occurs through means is well served. An uninterpreted scan of the text, however, could lead to the conclusion that God's eternal election is grounded on foreknowledge, indeed, foreknowledge of something in the individual human being.

On this issue, as well as on the general clarification of the text as a basis for the confessional statement, the *English Annotations* are precisely on point. We do not know the author of the annotation— Calamy suggested either John Downame or John Reading. Reflecting the exegesis of earlier Reformed commentators,[6] the annotation indicates in the first place that the address of Peter in verse 1 "to the strangers scattered throughout" various places in Asia Minor reads, in the Greek, "to the elect strangers," thus offering a foundation for the next clause, "elect according to the foreknowledge of God." The gloss on "elect," in the next clause, moreover, indicates that the primary sense of the word in this place is "sequestered and separated from the world." But more specifically, the annotation continues, by conferring John 15:19 and Revelation 17:14, the word "elect" is understood as synonymous with "called" and "faithful"—"so that here we are to understand by [elect] those who were effectually called, or who had obeyed the Gospel."[7] A similar reading, at considerably greater length, is found in the *Dutch Annotations*, where this election is identified as the temporal enactment of drawing people out of "the common heap of men" through calling according to the purpose of God.[8]

As to the problem of the word "foreknowledge," that annotation is also quite clear: we read, "*foreknowledge* Or, *preordination*; or, *foreappointment*; that is, as God had before decreed." There is, moreover, a strong echo of the earlier Reformed exegetical tradition on this issue: Calvin also has cautioned against the "sophists" who would read this text as an indication that election was grounded on a foreknowledge

6. Calvin, *Commentaries on I Peter*, 1:1–2, in loc. (*CTS 1 Peter*, 24).
7. *English Annotations* (1645), 1 Pet. 1:1–2, in loc.
8. *Dutch Annotations*, 1 Pet. 1:2, in loc.

of merit—foreknowledge here means simply that "God knew before the world was created whom he had elected for salvation."[9] Diodati and the *Dutch Annotations* offered a similar reading of the phrase.[10] So, too, do the *English Annotations* address the issue of means: "*through*] Here is set down the principall cause of their effectuall calling, *viz.* The sanctification of the Spirit."[11]

The other verses cited, Ephesians 1:4–5; 2:10, and 2 Thessalonians 2:13 also offer a sense of means of salvation, or at least secondary causality—a point noted by Featley's annotations. At Ephesians 1:5–6, we find a discussion of adoption as "the beginning and expectation" of the glory to come, and at Ephesians 2:10 Featley remarks that "we are Gods workmanship" not only in the first creation, but also in the second, which is our regeneration.[12] Diodati, perhaps more in the mind of the authors of the confession than the *English Annotations*, comments on the former verses that we are here shown three causes of salvation: the efficient cause, or good pleasure of God; the material cause, or Christ; and the final cause, the honor and glory of God. Calvin also understood these verses as referring to the causality of salvation.[13] On the latter text, Diodati comments that "good works are an effect and part of our salvation," worked in us by God and also worked by us, "God having by one and the same will and counsell, ordained the end of salvation, and the means to attain it."[14]

Featley's annotation on 2 Thessalonians 2:13 is very brief, noting that "sanctification of the spirit" could mean either the sanctification of the human spirit or heart through faith, or the sanctification "wrought" in human beings by the "Spirit of God."[15] There is, in other words, not much discussion offered in the *Annotations*, but there is firm ground for a conclusion to the effect that God not merely decrees election eternally, but also works it out temporally by means, namely adoption, regeneration, and sanctification.

9. Calvin, *Commentaries on I Peter*, 1:1–2, in loc. (*CTS 1 Peter*, 24).
10. Diodati, *Pious and Learned Annotations*, 1 Pet. 1:2, in loc.; cf. *Dutch Annotations*, 1 Pet. 1:2, in loc.
11. Gillespie, *Miscellany Questions*, 101.
12. *English Annotations* (1645), Eph. 2:10, in loc.
13. Calvin, *Commentary on Ephesians*, Eph. 1:5–6, in loc. (*CTS Ephesians*, 20–21).
14. Diodati, *Pious and Learned Annotations*, Eph. 2:10, in loc.
15. *English Annotations* (1645), 2 Thess. 2:13, in loc.

More foundation for the confessional use is found in other places in the exegetical tradition where the language of means and, indeed, secondary causality is found in the commentaries on these texts. Diodati is far more explicit on the precise issue addressed by the confession: "*Through sanctification* hereby is signified," he writes, "the order of secondary causes, and means of the accomplishment of the everlasting counsell of Gods election."[16] Calvin, with less explicit definition, had here noted that there was no reason to inquire into the eternal decree concerning election, given that we can inquire into our sanctification as proof.[17] The Geneva New Testament here similarly indicated that "election is known by these testimonies: Faith is gathered by sanctification: faith by that we accord unto the trueth: trueth, by calling, through the preaching of the Gospel: from whence wee come at length to a certaine hope of glorification."[18]

The results are similar when one examines the texts cited as a foundation for the limitation of the efficacy of Christ's work to the elect. The initial text brought to bear by the confession on this issue is John 17:9,[19] which includes the phrase, "I pray not for the world." John Ley's annotation is brief and blunt: at verse 6, "thine they were" he had indicated "by eternall election"—here, at verse 9, he simply comments, "not for reprobates."[20] The limitation placed by Christ in his own intercession in John 17:9, it should be noted, is one of the standard *loci* for arguing particular redemption (contrary to the rather silly argument found among some moderns that this exegesis implies, if only in Calvin's thought, a doctrine of "universal atonement").[21] The *English Annotations* are, thus, representative of a long exegetical tradition of the use of this text as an indicator of the limitation of Christ's redemptive work to the elect, as referenced and grounded in Christ's own intercession for those who are his. Calvin clearly understood the

16. Diodati, *Pious and Learned Annotations*, 2 Thess. 2:13, in loc.
17. Calvin, *Commentary on II Thessalonians*, 2:13, in loc. (*CTS Thessalonians*, 343).
18. *New Testament* [Beza-Tomson], 2 Thess. 2:13 n10.
19. Westminster Confession, 3.6.
20. *English Annotations* (1645), John 17:6, 9, in loc.
21. Cf. John Calvin, *Commentary on John*, 17:9, in loc. (*CTS John*, 2:172–73). Contra the rather odd argumentation in R. T. Kendall, *Calvin and English Calvinism to 1649* (Oxford: Clarendon Press, 1979), 16–17, where the limitation of Christ's intercession to the elect is contortedly explained as characteristic of a doctrine of universal atonement!

passage in this way;[22] so also did Beza, the Bezan annotations in the Tomson New Testament, and Diodati.[23]

The confessional summary of the issue of particular redemption, "Neither are any other redeemed by Christ, effectually called, justified, adopted, sanctified and saved; but the Elect only," not only makes the point of the limitation of divine intentionality in redemption to the elect, it also connects that limitation of intentionality with an order of salvation consisting in calling, justification, adoption, and sanctification. Accordingly, after John 17:9, the next text cited is Romans 8:28–39, the passage identified by much of the older exegetical tradition as the "golden chain." In the *English Annotations*, we are here dealing with the work of Daniel Featley, the lone Episcopalian who was pressed out of the Assembly early in its sessions and who was also eventually imprisoned for his objections to the Solemn League and Covenant—Episcopalian in polity and Royalist in politics, Featley was thoroughly Reformed in his theology: his more systematic or dogmatic efforts include a clear formulation of double predestination and an extended defense of the Reformed faith against the "Pelagians" of his time.[24] This Reformed understanding is evident in his approach to the last part of Romans 8, where he notes it to be a form of argument called a sorites or "golden chaine," in logic and rhetoric a movement toward a conclusion by way of a linked grouping of sub-arguments. He introduces the logical point, moreover, at verse 29 with reference to the words "for whom." Thus, in Featley's view, the movement from the eternal decree to the ultimate glorification of the elect is a "chaine . . . no link whereof can be unclinched, because the fastening thereof is the work of Gods omnipotence."[25] He also adds, at verse 30, that our salvation rests on "the death, the resurrection,

22. Calvin, *Commentary on John*, 17:9, in loc. (*CTS John*, 2:172–73).

23. Cf. Beza, *Annotationes in Novum Testamentum*, Jn. 17:6–9 in loc.; *New Testament* [Beza-Tomson], in loc., nn3, c, d; Diodati, *Pious and Learned Annotations*, in loc.

24. Daniel Featley, *The Hand-Maid to Private Devotion: the Second Part; Delivering the summe of saving knowledge, in 52 sections, answerable to the number of the Sundayes throughout the Yeere* (London: G. M. and R. B. for Nicholas Boorne, 1625); idem, *Parallelismus nov-antiqui erroris Pelagiarminiani* (London: Miles Flesher, 1626); idem, *A parallel: of nevv-old Pelgiarminian error* (London: Robert Milbourne, 1626); idem, *A second parallel* (London: J. Haviland for Robert Milbourne, 1626); idem, *Pelagius redivivus. Or Pelagius raked out of the ashes by Arminius and his schollers* (London: Robert Mylbourne, 1626).

25. *English Annotations* (1645), Rom. 8:29, in loc.

and the Almighty power of Jesus Christ," and that therefore, in the very conclusion of the argument of the second part of the epistle (which, he adds, is a "Treatise of justification"), God's children are given assurance of their unshakable salvation.[26] We have, therefore, not only a biblical text in general confirmation of the confessional teaching, but an exegetical argument on the text that confirms the actual argument in the confessional formula.

The 1645 *English Annotations* do not offer comment on John 6:64–65, 8:47, or 10:26, so that there is no indication of a direct referencing of the *Annotations* by the confession on these particular texts—although, given the additions found in subsequent editions of the *Annotations*, in which the project of commenting on the entire text of Scripture had been implemented, it is evident that the confession was rooted in a highly proximate exegetical tradition in its use of these verses as well. The 1657 annotation on 6:65 reads in part, paraphrasing Christ's words, "as if he said: therefore you are offended through unbelief, because my Father hath not given you faith to believe in me to your salvation." Similarly, at 8:47, the 1657 annotation indicates, "you beleeve not because you are not Gods sons"; and at 10:26, "For faith is the gift of God, which he gives onely to his. See Ephes. 2:8. Spiritual deafness toward the word of God is a certain effect of unbelief."[27]

Nor should the theological content of these additions be seen as the annotators' response to the confession: if we turn to other major commentaries and annotations written prior to the time of the confession, we easily find that the relationship of biblical text to confessional document had long been established in the older exegetical tradition. Calvin, for one, was quite certain that the message of John 6:65 was that grace was simply not "bestowed on all without exception," and that faith arises from the inward illumination or "secret revelation of the Spirit."[28] At John 8:47 and 10:26, Calvin explains the phrase "because you are not of my sheep" as the identification of those who refused to believe in Christ and his miracles as "reprobate" or having a

26. Ibid., Rom. 8:30, in loc.
27. *English Annotations* (1657), John 6:64; 8:47; 10:26, in loc.
28. Calvin, *Commentary on John*, 6:65, in loc. (*CTS John*, 1:276).

"reprobate mind."[29] Closer to the time of the confession, the marginal notes of the 1607 Tomson New Testament indicate that, according to John's gospel, faith is a gift only to the elect or "sheep";[30] so also do Diodati's annotations on all three texts offer similar exegetical support for the confessional understanding.[31]

The annotation at 1 John 2:19 briefly indicates that the phrase "they were not of us" refers to unbelievers who were in the church "in body onely, not in spirit," and that the faithful ought not to be perturbed by their falling away: "true believers . . . cannot fall away."[32] These latter texts do not speak as directly to the issue of particular redemption as does Romans 8:28 and following, but, as interpreted by various of the Reformed, do reinforce the sense of the confessional formula: in Calvin's view, the text confirms the "constancy" of God's election and the certainty of perseverance when God's calling is effectual—as it also testified to the absence of effectual calling among those who "fall away."[33] This reading carries over also into Beza's and Diodati's annotations as well as into the *English Annotations* and the citations found in the Westminster Standards.[34]

The Covenant of Works in the Confession and the *Annotations*

The doctrinal statements of the Westminster Confession concerning covenant and, in particular, the covenant of works have been the focus of a large amount of discussion, most of it of a highly theological or even dogmatic nature—and, oddly enough, given the biblical claims of the more negative of the writers, very little of it having a genuine exegetical dimension. When the Westminster Standards are examined in the light of various major antecedent thinkers and documents, however, a significant exegetical pattern emerges—not

29. Ibid., 8:47; 10:26, in loc. (*CTS John*, 1:354, 414).
30. *New Testament* [Beza-Tomson], John 6:63 n.14; 10:26.i.
31. Diodati, *Pious and Learned Annotations*, John 6:64; 8:47; 10:26, in loc.
32. *English Annotations* (1645), 1 John 2:19, in loc.
33. Calvin, *Commentary on 1 John*, 2:19, in loc. (*CTS 1 John*, 192).
34. Cf. Beza, *Annotationes in Novum Testamentum*, 1 John 2:19, in loc.; with Diodati, *Pious and Learned Annotations*, 1 John 2:19, in loc.

a pattern of proof-texting, but a pattern of exegetical inquiry that employed, quite strictly, the interpretive models of the sixteenth and seventeenth centuries in order to move from the text of Scripture to the doctrinal point.

In the light of this fundamental interpretive sensibility of the formulators of the doctrine and of the framers of the confession, it is of utmost importance to recognize that the doctrine of a prelapsarian covenant was in process of definition in the late sixteenth and seventeenth centuries and that the brief definition found in the Westminster Standards represents not a strict finalization of a dogma rigidly propounded, but a historical marker in an ongoing development. The formulators of the doctrine allowed for a significant flexibility in terms and definitions, and they consistently noted that the doctrine was not definitively offered by a single text in Scripture, but was, rather, a matter of inference.[35]

The initial formulators of the concept of a covenant of works—writers like Fenner, Polanus, and Perkins—focused their attention not only on Genesis 2:7, but also on various passages from the Pauline letters, notably Romans and Galatians. Fenner's exposition of the doctrine cites Genesis 2:17, Romans 3:19–20, 7:7–11, and 11:32, Galatians 3:8–10, 15–17, 23, and 5:23.[36] Polanus looks to Genesis 2:17, Galatians 3:19–20, and 7:7–11,[37] and Perkins emphasizes Galatians 4:24–25,[38] but notes such texts as Romans 10:5 and 7:14 as foundational to the doctrine.[39] Rollock focused his attention on Genesis 2:17, Galatians 3:10 and 12, and Romans 10:5 as grounds of the

35. See Ernest F. Kevan, *The Grace of Law: A Study in Puritan Theology* (London: Carey Kingsgate Press, 1964), 111–12.

36. Dudley Fenner, *Sacra theologia, sive Veritas quae est secundum pietatem* (London, 1585), 2.2(88).

37. Amandus Polanus von Polansdorf, *Partitiones theologiae christianae*, pars. 1–2 (London: Edmund Bollifant, 1591), 1.33(53); in translation, *The Substance of the Christian Religion* (London: R. F. for Iohn Oxenbridge, 1595), 1.33(96–97).

38. William Perkins, *A Commentarie, or Exposition upon the five first Chapters of the Epistle to the Galatians . . . continued with a Supplement upon the sixth Chapter, by Ralfe Cudworth* (London: John Legatt, 1617), Gal. 4:24–25, 6:8 in loc. (303–7, 502); note that latter discussion belongs to the portion of the text written by Cudworth.

39. William Perkins, *A Golden Chaine*, in *The Workes of . . . Mr. William Perkins*, 3 vols. (Cambridge: John Legatt, 1612–19), 1:32 (cap. 19), citing Jer. 31:31–33; Rom. 10:5; 1 Tim. 1:5; Luke 16:27; and Rom. 7:14 by way of arguing the distinction and the nature of the two covenants.

doctrine of the covenant of works.[40] What is evident in all four of these early covenant thinkers is that the doctrine of a prelapsarian covenant arises not out of a single statement of Scripture, certainly not out of a potentially controverted text like Hosea 6:7, but out of a complex of texts examined in their theological interrelationship.

In the generation of writers immediately preceding the Westminster Assembly, there was both a clear formulation of the doctrine of the covenants of works and grace, and the recognition, as John Ball put it, that the full and specific doctrine of a covenant of works cannot be found *totidem syllabis* in any one place in the Scriptures. "The neerest we come to it," in Ball's view, "is *Rom.* 3:27, the Law of works opposed to the Law of faith; which holds out as much as the Covenant of workes, and the Covenant of Grace."[41] Anthony Burgess notes, echoing sentiments similar to those of Ball, that "this covenant with *Adam* in the state of innocency, is more obscurely laid down, than the covenant of grace after the fall," given that later covenants are expressly identified as such whereas the prelapsarian covenant "must onely be gathered by deduction and consequence."[42] Burgess also indicates that we ought not to be so "rigid" as to demand "expresse places" where God's relationship with Adam is called a covenant inasmuch as what is drawn by necessary consequence from Scripture is as true as Scripture itself. After Genesis 2, where a covenant can be concluded from the promises and stipulations made by God with Adam, the doctrine of a covenant with Adam arises perhaps most clearly from the discussion of Adam and Christ in Romans 5, where salvation appears as an alternative federal arrangement made in Christ.[43]

Of interest here is that all of these writers understood the primary ground of the covenant of works, apart from Genesis 2:17, as Pauline and as found in Romans and Galatians. None of these writers looked to Hosea 6:7, although they surely knew of its long

---

40. Robert Rollock, *Quaestiones et responsiones aliquot de foedere Dei, deque sacramewnto quod foederis Dei sigillum est* (Edinburgh: Henricus Charteris, 1596), fol. A3 verso–A4 recto.

41. Ball, *Treatise of the Covenant of Grace*, 1.2(9).

42. Anthony Burgess, *Vindiciae legis, or, A vindication of the morall law and the covenants, from the errours of Papists, Arminians, Socinians, and more especially, Antinomians. In XXX. lectures, preached at Laurence-Jury, London* (London: James Young, for Thomas Underhill, 1647), 123.

43. Burgess, *Vindiciae legis*, 123–24.

tradition of covenantal interpretation.[44] A similar pattern of argument will emerge in our examination of the texts cited in the Westminster Confession and catechisms—and the rationale for this pattern and for the doctrine itself will become evident in our examination of the exegetical background to the proof-texting of the confession. Perhaps most evident are the concerns for a genuinely biblical formulation and the practice of building that foundation by the collation of texts as places or seats of doctrinal argumentation.[45]

By way of introducing the issue of the confessional reading of the covenant of works and its exegetical background, it is important to note that the chapter in which the doctrine of the covenant of works is contained is entitled broadly "Of Gods Covenant with Man," and begins with a general statement of how covenant serves the divine purpose before entering into discussion of God's particular covenants:

> The distance between God and Creatures is so great, that although reasonable Creatures do owe obedience unto him as Creator, yet they could never have any fruition of him as their Blessednesse and Reward, but by some voluntary condescension on Gods part, which he hath been pleased to expresse by way of Covenant [a: Isa. 40:13–17; Job 9:32–33; 1 Sam. 2:25; Ps. 113:5–6; 100:2–3; Job 22:2–3; 35:7–8; Luke 17:10; Acts 17:24–25].[46]

This introductory statement is clearly intended to cover both covenants, works and grace—in effect, ruling out any notion of an absolutely merited eternal reward for humanity even under the covenant of works. There is no possibility of final blessedness and eternal reward apart from "some voluntary condescension on Gods part."[47]

Having stated this common ground of the two covenants, the confession then proceeds to define the covenant of works:

44. Cf. Richard A. Muller, "The Covenant of Works and the Stability of Divine Law in Seventeenth-Century Reformed Orthodoxy: A Study in the Theology of Herman Witsius and Wilhelmus à Brakel," *Calvin Theological Journal* 29 (1994): 89–90.

45. Cf. Muller, *Post Reformation Reformed Dogmatics*, 2:7.4(C.5); 7.5(B.1–3).

46. Westminster Confession, 7.1.

47. Note that the presence of divine grace prior to the fall was a fundamental assumption of most of the Reformed thinkers of the era: see Kevan, *Grace of Law*, 112, 113–26, passim; cf. Muller, "The Covenant of Works and the Stability of Divine Law," 91–93.

The first Covenant made with Man, was a Covenant of Works [b: Gal. 3:12], wherein Life was promised to Adam, and in him to his posterity [c: Rom. 10:5; Rom 5:12–20], upon condition of perfect and personall obedience [d: Gen. 2:17; Gal. 3:10].[48]

The language of the catechisms is notably different from that of the confession. Both refer to the prelapsarian covenant as a "Covenant of life," and the Larger Catechism adds, "of which the Tree of Life was a pledge." The biblical proofs cited in the catechisms are similar to those of the confession—the Shorter Catechism citing Galatians 2:17, the Larger Catechism adding Romans 10:5, with reference to the covenant of life, and Genesis 2:9 with reference to the tree of life, specifically reflecting Rollock's (rather than Perkins's or Ball's) sense of the biblical foundations of the doctrine.[49] Beyond the differences in citation, there is a common thread of biblical argument; all of the writers and the confessional documents as well move from the obedience required of Adam in Genesis 2:17 to a series of Pauline tests in order to argue the doctrine.

It is first worth noting one potential proof-text that is missing from the confession and catechisms. As has been observed in a recent study, the confession does not at this point cite Hosea 6:7—"Like Adam [or, "like man"] they transgressed the covenant."[50] Nor, indeed, do the catechisms or the confession cite collateral texts that are often conjoined with Hosea 6:7 to argue that its reference to "Adam" ought not to be read as a generic reference to humanity generally, but as a specific reference to the first human being, namely Job 31:33, "If I covered my transgressions as Adam"; and Isaiah 43:27, "Thy first father hath sinned. . . ." I will not here relate the issue of the history of exegesis of Hosea 6:7, except to note that the absence of the text from the confession in no way implies that the prior exegetical tradition lacked the understanding of the text as referencing a prelapsarian covenant with Adam. Indeed, the text had been understood as a reference to

48. Westminster Confession, 7.2.
49. Larger Catechism, Q.21; but cf. Q.30, where the term "covenant of works" appears; Shorter Catechism, Q.12.
50. David A. Weir, *The Origins of the Federal Theology in Sixteenth-Century Reformation Thought* (Oxford: Clarendon Press, 1990), 14–15.

an Adamic covenant throughout the earlier history of exegesis and had, in fact, been interpreted in that way in a series of commentaries known to the authors of the confession, namely, in the *Statenvertaling* annotations, in Diodati, and in the *English Annotations*.[51]

This datum is slightly curious—the authors of the confession could have cited Hosea 6:7 as a basic proof of the covenant of works, confident in the fact that a reader of the confession needed only to look to the *Annotations* commissioned by Parliament to find the text interpreted in support of the confession! Why, then, did the confession's authors cite other texts in support of their doctrinal point? Unfortunately, they do not tell us. But we can surmise—indeed, there are perhaps as many as three reasons. First, the interpretation of Hosea 6:7 was disputed. Second, related to the first point, although the *English Annotations* favored reading the text as a reference to the covenant of works, the interpretation was referenced to the marginal reading of the AV and not on the line of the text, which read, "Like man. . . ." Third, although Hosea 6:7 did, potentially, offer a brief testimony to the existence of a prelapsarian covenant, it did not identify that covenant as consisting in a requirement of obedience or "works." The doctrine of the covenant of works, as we have just noted, was defined by a significant number of Reformed thinkers in the era prior to the Westminster Assembly primarily with Pauline texts, collated to Genesis 2:17 and connected with the notion of covenant as the form of the divine condescension necessary to any proper relationship between God and human beings. And it is those Pauline texts plus Genesis 2:17 that are cited in the confession.

Some insight into the exegetical background of the confession is available from the *English Annotations* on the texts cited, namely Genesis 2; Galatians 3; and Romans 5 and 10. The first of these texts, Genesis 2, is cited in all three of the standards, verse 17 being cited in all three documents, verse 9 in the Larger Catechism. Reference to Genesis 2 occurs in the confession and catechisms not at the point of identifying an initial covenant of works or life, but rather at the point of indicating the promise of life to Adam and his posterity "upon condition of perfect and personall obedience." That formal

---

51. Cf. *English Annotations* (1645), Hos. 6:7, in loc., with Muller, *PRRD*, 2:436–41.

issue should govern our sense of the relationship of the standards to the exegesis of the day in general and to the *English Annotations* in particular. The author of the annotations on Genesis, John Ley, was a member of the Assembly, albeit not of the subcommittee that drafted the confession. His annotations on Genesis 2 indicate that the prohibition pronounced by God concerning the tree of knowledge "witnessed his owne originall right to dispose of his creatures . . . and put them to the practice of submission to their maker," through a command concerning an otherwise "indifferent" thing, offering life in return for obedience, death as the penalty for disobedience.[52] There is no specific mention of covenant in the 1645 annotation, but there is surely indication of the support given by the exegetical tradition for the primary argument of the confession, namely the requirement of obedience.

The 1645 *Annotations* also support the Larger Catechism's understanding of the tree of life, albeit not dogmatically or reductionistically: we read that the tree was so called for either of two reasons—on the one hand, it may have been called the tree of life because it could have afforded such nourishment to Adam and Eve that, had they not sinned, they would have been preserved from disease; on the other,

> because it Sacramentally signified, that if a man persisted in obedience to God, he should continue in health and strength in that place, and state, until thence (without disease or death) he were taken up to the place and state of everlasting life in the Paradise above, as Enoch was, Gen. 5:24, and Elijah, 2 Kings 2:11 and (God who gave it the name foreseeing both mans misery, and his remedy by redemption in Christ) it might be so called as a type and figure of him, who brought life and immortality . . . whence he might (as he is) be named the *tree of life*, Revel. 22:2.[53]

The additional annotations of 1655, in which Gataker had a hand, highlight the sacramental understanding by commenting briefly, "*tree of life* because naturaly much, but sacramentaly more."[54] Whereas

---

52. *English Annotations* (1645), Gen. 2:9, in loc.
53. Ibid.
54. *Choice Observations*, Gen. 2:9, in loc.

the catechism states the point briefly, the annotation is somewhat more expansive—notably, where the catechism speaks of the tree as a sign of the covenant, the annotation goes a bit further and identifies it as a sacramental sign, a point typical of the exegetical tradition reaching back at least to Augustine and characteristic of the covenant theology of the seventeenth century. The annotation also supports, albeit indirectly, the confessional implication of a graciousness on God's part even in the covenant of works; and it supports also the catechetical interest in identifying this prelapsarian arrangement as a covenant of life. Again, there is no specific reference to a covenant here, although it is the case that both elsewhere in the *English Annotations* and throughout the broader exegetical and theological tradition, sacraments, including the trees in the garden, are understood as covenantal signs.[55]

The annotations on the Pauline Epistles are from the pen of Daniel Featley. Galatians 3 is certainly a major covenant *locus* in sixteenth- and seventeenth-century exegesis and, in many of the commentaries, a place where the issue of two covenants, works and grace is raised and debated. As noted previously, the Royalist Episcopalian Featley was, in theology, strongly Reformed—and, although his *Summe of Saving Knowledge* does not include a discussion of the covenants, his exegesis, as found in the *English Annotations*, does indicate his interest in the doctrine. The annotation on Galatians 3:12 is brief, setting up the antithesis between justification under the law and justification through faith:

> *the law is not of faith*] The Law promiseth life to all that keep it, and therefore if it be kept it justifieth and giveth life; but the Scripture attributing righteousness and life to faith, taketh it from the Law; seeing faith justifieth by imputation of anothers righteousnesse, and the Law by performing the work in our own person.[56]

The elaboration of the promise of life to all who keep the law—in the confessional language, "to Adam and . . . his posterity"—rests on Romans 10:5 and 5:12–20.

55. Cf. John Calvin, *Institutio christianae religionis* (Geneva: Stephanus, 1559), 4.14.18.
56. *English Annotations* (1645), Gal. 3:12, in loc.

76

On the former of these texts, Featley's annotation reads, "such is the condition of the law, that he that doeth the works of the law shall live; but cursed is he that confirmeth not all of the works of the law to do them, Deut. 27:26."[57] Other commentaries in the earlier Reformed exegetical tradition, notably the *Dutch Annotations*, offer similar juxtapositions of law and faith as mutually exclusive paths to fellowship with God: "For the Law promiseth life, not to them who will be justified by Faith, but who perfectly keep the Law . . . which nevertheless no man doth, nor can do."[58] Rollock's and Piscator's readings are nearly identical.[59]

The second of these citations, Romans 5:12–20, points toward the Pauline Adam-Christ comparison, understood by Featley as confirming the doctrine that Adam was made the "head and root . . . of all mankind" as well as the doctrine of original sin.[60] Neither here nor in the annotations on Galatians 3:12 and Romans 10:5 does Featley use the phrase "covenant of works"—nor, incidentally, did Rollock expand on the covenant of works in his commentaries on these texts, despite their rather prominent citation as proofs in his *De foedere*, and despite the *locus* on the two covenants folded into his exegesis of Romans 8.[61] Beza here not only draws the parallels of Adam and Christ, law and faith, but also adds that Adam understood the "law of nature."[62]

Featley's reading, moreover, has much in common with Burgess's use of Romans 5 in connection with the interpretation of Genesis 2:17 as indicating a prelapsarian covenant. Burgess indicates that one confirmation of the presence of a covenant in Genesis 2 is the inclusion of Adam's posterity in his sin and their being made subject to the same punishment, as made clear by Paul—"the Apostle *Rom.* 5 makes all men in *Adam,* as the godly are in Christ: now beleevers come to receive of Christ, not from a naturall necessity, because they

---

57. *English Annotations* (1645), Rom. 10:5, in loc.

58. *Dutch Annotations*, Rom. 10:5, in loc., collating with Rom. 3:9ff.

59. Robert Rollock, *Analysis dialectica . . . in Pauli Apostoli Epistolam ad Romanos* (Edinburgh: Robert Waldegrave, 1593), 10:5, in loc. (246–47); Johannes Piscator, *Analysis logica omnium Epistolarum Pauli* (London: George Bishop, 1608), Rom. 10:5, in loc. (125).

60. *English Annotations* (1645), Rom. 5:12, in loc.

61. Rollock, *Analysis . . . in Epistolam ad Romanos*, 161–63.

62. Beza, *Annotationes in Novum Testamentum*, Rom. 5:13–14, in loc.

have that human nature which Christ took upon him, (for so all should be saved) but by a federal agreement."[63]

Although Galatians 3:20 is not among the verses cited in the confession's selective referencing of Galatians chapter 3, the annotation offered by the *English Annotations* in 1645 is quite significant to the doctrine of the covenant of works:

> *Now a mediatour is not a* mediatour *of one*] Either the meaning is, a Mediatour is not a Mediatour of one partie, but betwixt two, and these disagreeing; this sheweth that at the giving of the Law there was a difference and a distance between God and us, which difference grew from this, that we were transgressours of the Law: or the meaning is, a Mediatour is not a Mediatour of one covenant onely, but as well of the Covenant of grace as of the Covenant of works.[64]

Featley justifies his conclusion that the text probably references the covenant of works exegetically by an appeal to Christ as the scope of all Scripture:

> *but God is one*] In these words he taketh away an objection lest any man might say, that sometimes by consent of the parties which have made a Covenant something is added to the Covenant; or former Covenants are broken: this, saith the Apostle, cometh not to passe in God, who is alwaies one and the self same, and like to himself, and hath the same scope and end in both his Covenants; for Christ is the end of the Law: or that God is still the same in holding a distance between himself and transgressours, if they seek to be justified by the Law.[65]

Clearly, the former sense of the phrase "not a mediatour of one" as meaning not a mediator of one party is the usual reading—and it is the reading, certainly, that appears in most of the commentaries of the era as the sole reading of the text, notably the commentaries of

63. Cf. Burgess, *Vindiciae legis*, 124; note the Adam-Christ parallel, 122.
64. *English Annotations* (1645), Gal. 3:20, in loc.
65. Ibid.

Rollock,[66] Piscator,[67] Perkins,[68] the *Dutch Annotations*,[69] Diodati,[70] and Dickson.[71]

The christological reading of the covenant of works is not, however, a curious feature of the *English Annotations*. There is an interesting anticipation of the point in Calvin's commentary on the text: Calvin notes that the common exposition of the text is that Christ is the Mediator between "two parties" in dispute. He does not, however, take the "two parties" in the usual later sense as God and the human race. Rather, he comments that "Christ is not a Mediator of one, because, in respect of outward character, there is a difference of condition among those with whom, through his mediation, God enters into covenant," namely the Jews under the Old Testament and Christ under the New Testament.[72] And from two years prior to the publication of the *English Annotations*, we meet with a view much like that of Featley, with reference to other texts, in the famous sermons of Tobias Crisp, *Christ Alone Exalted* (1643):

There are two main generall covenants God enters into with men; the one is called the first covenant, *the old covenant*, the covenant of works: it stood upon these terms: *doe this and live*. The other is called a *new Covenant*, by the prophet *Jeremy*; and, by the apostle, in the 8th chap. to the *Hebrews*, it is called a better covenant, a covenant of grace. As for the first, the old covenant, the covenant of works, which stood upon these termes, *doe this and live*. It is very probable, if not certain, that Christ was this first covenant unto men, even the covenant of works. For, however it be not a covenant of grace, as the second and new covenant is: yet it may, in some sense, be

66. Robert Rollock, *Analysis Logica in Epistolam Pauli ad Galatas* (London: Felix Kyngston, 1602), Gal. 3:20, in loc. (63).

67. Piscator, *Analysis . . . Epistolarum Pauli*, Gal. 3:20, in loc. (415).

68. William Perkins, *A Commentarie, or Exposition upon the five first Chapters of the Epistle to the Galatians* (London: John Legatt, 1617), 3:20 (192).

69. *Dutch Annotations*, Gal. 3:20, in loc.

70. Diodati, *Pious and Learned Annotations*, Gal. 3:20, in loc.

71. David Dickson, *Expositio Analytica omnium Apostolicarum Epistolarum* (Glasgow, George Anderson, 1647), Gal. 3:20, in loc. (322); idem, *An Exposition of all St. Pauls Epistles, together with an Explanation of those other Epistles of the Apostles, St. James, Peter, John, & Jude* (London: R. I. for Francis Eglesfield, 1659), Gal. 3:20, in loc. (99).

72. Calvin, *Commentaries on Galatians*, 3:20, in loc. (*CTS Galatians*, 103).

called a covenant of grace, in reference unto other creatures: For all creatures are under this tie, *to doe this*, that is, what their part is which God hath imposed upon them: Yet no creature hath this privilege of grace, that in doing this, he should live. . . . Proverbs 8:31. You shall see the ground of this Covenant. When the Lord made all things in the world, *wisedome*, which is *Christ*, there tels us, that *she was the delight of the Father, and her whole delight was with the sons of men*."[73]

By contrast, Ferguson's commentary on Galatians 3:20, published in 1659, probably registers an awareness of the *English Annotations* on the point and disagrees. In Ferguson's view, the covenant of works between God and Adam had no mediator given that, prior to the fall, God and man were in agreement, in effect, "were one"—and a mediator is not a mediator of one! The text does imply a covenant between two disparate parties inasmuch as it refers to the necessity of a mediator, but the reference, in Ferguson's view, can be only to the covenant of grace.[74]

What can we conclude in general about the relationship of the confession to the exegetical tradition in the case of the covenant of works and, from that conclusion, about the early Reformed understanding of the reasons for arguing a covenant of works? First, the confession related to the exegetical tradition in much the same way as the early formulators of the two covenant model—the foundation of the doctrine was primarily Pauline, collated to Genesis 2:17. Second, beyond the sacramental understanding of the trees in the garden and the biblical datum of a requirement of obedience placed on Adam, the fundamental concept of a prelapsarian covenant of works (or of "nature" or "life") was grounded in the Pauline antitheses of Adam and Christ, law and faith. In other words, the documents indicate that the interrelated series, Christ, faith, covenant of grace, was juxtaposed with Adam, law, and the covenant of works, with the prelapsarian covenant supplied as the

73. Tobias Crisp, *Christ Alone Exalted. In fourteene Sermons* (London: Richard Bishop, 1643), sermon 6 (155–56).
74. James Ferguson, *A Brief Exposition of the Epistles of Paul to the Galatians and Ephesians* (Edinburgh: Christopher Higgins, 1659), Gal. 3:20, in loc. (48).

necessary conclusion demanded by the collation of texts. In effect, the confession at this point exemplifies its own statement of the Reformed method of interpretation—that Christian doctrine is to be either grounded upon the express statements of Scripture or drawn from those statements as a "good and necessary consequence."[75] This had been the way in which the early orthodox Reformed theologians had developed their understanding of the prelapsarian covenant on the basis of Genesis 2:17 and various Pauline texts—and it remained the method of the confession and catechisms.[76]

Conclusions

The correlations that we have seen between the citations of Scripture in the Westminster Confession of Faith and the exegetical tradition represented in part by the *English Annotations* are numerous and specific. As indicated in the introductory remarks, we were not led by the documents or by their authors to expect a neat one-to-one correlation, as if the confessional standards were written with consistent, precise reference to the *English Annotations,* or as if the various strata of the *Annotations* evidence a checking of theological positions against the confession. The relationship between the documents is far more subtle and variegated than that. On the one hand, the pattern of citing biblical proofs found in the confessional standards was not a form of rank proof-texting, as has sometimes been alleged of the Westminster Standards and of the theological works of the seventeenth-century orthodox in general. Rather, the confession and the catechisms cite texts by way of referencing an exegetical tradition reaching back, in many cases, to the fathers of the church in the first five centuries of Christianity and, quite consistently, reflecting the path of biblical interpretation belonging to the Reformed tradition as it developed in the sixteenth century and in the beginning of the seventeenth. On the other hand, the *English Annotations* stand in that tradition, in conscious reliance on the work of predecessors like Beza, Diodati, and the Dutch

75. Westminster Confession, 1.6.
76. Cf. the discussion in *PRRD*, 4:7.4 (C.5).

annotators of the *Statenvertaling* and, accordingly, frequently serve as an indicator of the ways in which biblical texts were interpreted at the time of the Westminster Assembly.

Our examination of the correlations between the confession and the exegetical tradition indicates that—at least in the places examined—the authors of the Westminster Standards could be confident that their doctrinal statements did indeed reflect the teaching of Scripture and, quite specifically, that the added biblical proofs provided an avenue into the teaching of Scripture for the readers of the confession and catechisms. In addition, it is also the case that the *English Annotations* consistently provide a guide to Scripture that, given its rootage in the Reformed exegetical tradition, typically supports the confessional statements and often explicitly grounds the confession and catechisms with a series of readings either from which the confessional conclusion could be drawn or from which the confession's doctrine arose directly.

PART 2

THE DIRECTORY FOR PUBLIC WORSHIP

Rowland S. Ward

5

Background and Principles[1]

The Westminster Assembly

Some of our great past milestones have collected about them a variety of myths. There are those who think that the King James Version of the Bible is beyond criticism as the production of providentially guided and extraordinarily saintly men. They do not seem aware that it was indeed the production of scholarly men, but men who were not generally Puritans, but often high and even dry Anglicans. Their work did not displace the Geneva Bible, beloved by the common people, for a generation. In the lengthy preface found in library editions, the KJV translators rejected the kind of status given their work by later admirers.

Similarly, the Westminster Assembly is often thought of as an Assembly of keen Presbyterians who had to suffer the irritant of some dissenting brethren of the Independent way and a few Erastians. In fact Richard Baxter (1615–91), a great pastor but not a good theologian, and not a member of the Assembly, observed concerning the times of the Assembly:

> Any Man that was for a Spiritual serious way of worship (though he were for moderate Episcopacy and Liturgy) and that lived according

1. A lecture given at Westminster Theological Seminary, Philadelphia, on October 21, 2004, on the occasion of the seventy-fifth anniversary of the seminary, revised for publication.

to his Profession, was commonly called a *Presbyterian*, as formerly he was called a *Puritan*, unless he joined himself to *Independents*, *Anabaptists*, or some other Sect which might afford him a more odious Name.[2]

If Baxter is correct, then these "Presbyterians," though notable for both learning and spirituality, were not necessarily Presbyterian as we understand the term. All but one had been episcopally ordained. Further, the Assembly, like Dort or Nicea before it, was not a proper synod, but an assembly created by the civil authority to advise it. Unlike the Scots, the 121 ministers[3] and 30 parliamentarians who were members of the Assembly, though the average attendance was only sixty to eighty, had no extended experience of organized Presbyterianism. Their degree of knowledge of and commitment to it varied, as did their attitudes to forms of worship. The English Puritans were not agreed in every aspect of church life any more than are all the ministers of any orthodox denomination of even moderate size today. Attitudes to churchmanship and even hermeneutical method existed, so that the more biblicist tended to independency. In the wider interest of the church and people the godly were ready to take the opportunity of bringing about a more thorough reformation, particularly to deal with the Prelatic party and associated evils and abuses in worship. Presbyterianism offered a national form for the church that was attractive to many. They saw the existing Episcopal structure as inimical to the gospel, and Independency as a recipe for chaos. Thus, many might have been content with a reformed episcopacy that served the interests of the gospel. But times were dark for England, and the kingdom in the north was ready to help. The six Scots at Westminster were not members of the Assembly, but treaty commissioners, representatives of the Church of Scotland and the Scottish nation, charged to secure the commitments to uniformity made in the Solemn League and Covenant of 1643. The Scots were not Episcopalians but Presbyterians,

2. Matthew Sylvester, ed., *Reliquiae Baxterianae, or Mr Richard Baxter's Narrative of the Most Memorable Passages of his Life and Times* (London 1696), 278.
3. The exact number is hard to determine. The initial number nominated by Parliament totaled 121, but about 20 were appointed to replace those who died or who did not participate. A total of forty-one members plus the six Scots and several others are profiled in William S. Barker, *Puritan Profiles* (Fearn: Mentor, 1996).

very convinced and experienced Presbyterians. That's the broad-brush picture of the Westminster Assembly.[4]

The Origin and Public History of the Directory

We speak of worship wars today. There were worship wars then as well as civil war, and in fact the two were closely related. The need for the religious question to be settled was pressing. The English were familiar with the Book of Common Prayer 1559/1604, which was mandated by law. In practice there had been a certain degree of variation in adherence to it as circumstances allowed, but the prevailing Prelatic party in England under Archbishop Laud was bent on strict conformity, and on extending it to Scotland. The Scots were familiar with the 1564 Book of Common Order derived from the 1556 Book of Prayers used by Knox and others in Geneva. It was commonly called Knox's Liturgy, although it was really a "discretionary Liturgy"[5] with a generally fixed outline and space for free prayer. Sample prayers were provided, but the rubrics allowed for prayer "like in effect," or as God "shall move his heart."[6] In short, the Scots were largely similar in their form of worship to other Reformed churches in Europe, while England had a liturgy that did not give discretion, and that had various features that had proved unhelpful to gospel ministry.

I find it surprising that so well informed a writer as Horton Davies suggests that the Puritans probably were not aware of "the cleavage between themselves and John Calvin" and how their viewpoint differed

4. R. S. Paul, *The Assembly of the Lord* (Edinburgh: T & T Clark, 1985), 101–32, gives a well-informed survey of the religious parties in the 1640s. The earlier study by J. R. DeWitt, *Jus Divinum: The Westminster Assembly and the Divine Right of Church Government* (Kampen: Kok, 1969), is defective at this point, as DeWitt later acknowledged in John L. Carson & David W. Hall, eds., *To Glorify and Enjoy God* (Edinburgh: Banner of Truth, 1994), 150.

5. G. W. Sprott, *The Book of Common Order* (Edinburgh: William Blackwood & Sons, 1901), xxi. Note James Bannerman's comment: "It must be perfectly clear to any man who reads the Book of Common Order with any attention, that to call it a Liturgy in the strict and technical sense of that term, is a mere misuse of words." *The Church of Christ* ([1869] Edinburgh: Banner of Truth, 1974) 2:418.

6. A good case for this understanding is in A. F. Mitchell, *The Reformation in Scotland* (Edinburgh: William Blackwood & Sons, 1900), 123–43. It should be noted that a majority of Scottish parishes had "readers," not regular ministers, during the sixteenth century.

from the practice of other Reformed churches.[7] The facts are otherwise, and Davies really undermines his assertion on his page 112. The idea that the English Puritans were unfamiliar with the history and liturgical practice of other Reformed churches is inherently improbable given the educational attainments of the Puritans, the availability of Calvin's writings in England, Scottish contacts, the use of Latin throughout Europe (which facilitated exchange of information), and the controversies in which the Puritans were involved. Puritan writings specifically show that familiarity, including the issues at Frankfurt in Calvin's time, and his description of some aspects of the English liturgy as "tolerable fooleries."[8] The Puritans were aware that ministers were not tightly tied to set forms of prayer in churches such as the Dutch and Genevan.[9]

A new service book for Scotland was given royal proclamation in December 1636. It is commonly known as "Laud's Liturgy" (after the Archbishop of Canterbury), and was a fixed liturgy from which a minister could not vary without risk of being removed from his office. The Scottish bishops were involved in its preparation, but not the General Assembly, which had not been convened since 1618. Laud's Liturgy reflected the views of the king and the Prelatic party. It was based on the English Prayer Book, differed from it in some respects, but tended to a Romeward direction in the view of many. The attempted introduction of this liturgy in July 1637 not only provoked the famous stool-throwing incident by Jenny Geddes at Saint Giles' Edinburgh, but also contributed to the summoning of the great

7. *The Worship of the English Puritans* (Westminster: Dacre Press, 1948), 48. J. I. Packer, among others, cites Davies approvingly in *Among God's Giants:The PuritanVision of the Christian Life* (Eastbourne: Kingsway, 1991), 327.

8. Smectymnuus, *A Vindication* (London, 1641), 13–14.

9. Ibid., 40–41. Calvin's *Forme of prayers* had been translated by William Huycke and published at London in 1550. The use of common forms of prayer in the Dutch churches "went out of use towards the close of the seventeenth century" although retained for the sacraments, according to Charles W. Baird, *The Presbyterian Liturgies, Historical Sketches* (Grand Rapids: Baker, 1957), 209. Editions of Knox's *Forme of Prayers* were republished in London in October 1643 under the title *The Reformation of the Discipline and Service of the Church according to the best Reformed Churches . . . Humbly presented to the High Court of Parliament,* and in a more original form (includes original preface and fewer prayers) in 1644 under the title, *The Setled* [sic] *Order of Church Government, Liturgie and Discipline . . . according to the Forme published by the Assembly of the Kirk of Scotland . . . Most humbly presented to the learned Assembly of Divines . . .* [Wing no. S2731].

Glasgow General Assembly in 1638, with Alexander Henderson as moderator, when the National Covenant was signed and Presbyterianism restored. Gillespie wrote his masterly *A Dispute Against English Popish Ceremonies obtruded on the Church of Scotland* against Laud's Liturgy in mid-1637 when he was not yet 25, and Baillie published similar works in 1640 and 1641.[10]

Many in England were concerned for their church and nation. Bishop Joseph Hall issued *An Humble Remonstrance* in 1640 in the interest of a strict liturgy and Episcopal Church government. Five Presbyterians responded in 1641 with *An Answer to a Book Entitled An Humble Remonstrance*, and soon after *A vindication of the answer*. Among other things they noted: "But we think, nay, we know, that some few Prelates by their over rigorous pressing of the Service-book and ceremonies, have made more Separatists, than all the Preachers disaffected to the Ceremonies in England."[11]

Civil war broke out in England in August 1642.[12] The English Parliament sought help from the Scots in their conflict with the king. Among the letters received by the Church of Scotland Assembly in August 1643 was one signed by more than seventy ministers that described "the bleeding condition of your poor distressed Brethren in England" as a result of the anti-Christian faction of "Papists and

10. *Ladensium Autokatakrisis, the Canterburians Self-Conviction* (Edinburgh, April 1640). Note also *A Parallel or Briefe Comparison of the Liturgie with the Masse-book . . .* (London: Thomas Paine, 1641). These have been assessed by a recognized Episcopal historian as "mere hysterical rants . . . not worthy of serious consideration, except as illustrating the inflamed state of public opinion generally." Gordon Donaldson, *The Making of the Scottish Prayer Book of 1637* (Edinburgh, 1954), 71. Philip Schaff is more candid (*The Creeds of Christendom*, 1:712): "Laud was of small stature and narrow mind, but strong will and working power, hot and irascible in temper, ungracious and unpopular in manner, ignorant of human nature, a zealous ritualist, a pedantic disciplinarian, and an overbearing priest . . . His chief zeal was directed to the establishment of absolute outward uniformity in religion as he understood it, without regard to the rights of conscience and private judgment. His religion consisted of High-Church Episcopalianism and Arminianism in the nearest possible approach to Rome, which he admired and loved, and the furthest possible distance from Geneva, which he hated and abhorred."

11. Smectymnuus, *A Vindication of the Answer to the Humble Remonstrance* (London, 1641), 38. The authors were Stephen Marshall, Edmund Calamy, Thomas Young, Mathew Newcomen and William Spurstow. Their initials formed "Smectymnuus."

12. The English Civil Wars were to cost perhaps one hundred thousand lives, one in fifty-seven of the total population (say 10 percent of the adult male population)—compared to one in fifty for the American Civil War (620,000 out of 31 million). The Thirty Years' War (1618–48) was still raging in Europe, costing several million lives.

Prelates." Robert Baillie records, "The letter of the private Divines was so lamentable, that it drew tears from many."[13] The Scots proposed what was called the Solemn League and Covenant with its aim of bringing about a uniformity for the church in England, Ireland, and Scotland "according to the Word of God and the example of the best Reformed churches." The English House of Commons accepted it in September. This price for Scottish military assistance resulted in the Assembly of Divines, which had commenced its work on July 1, 1643, abandoning revision of the Thirty-nine Articles and giving immediate attention to the practical issues of church government and public worship. On December 2, 1643, a subcommittee consisting of Stephen Marshall, Charles Herle, Herbert Palmer, Thomas Young, and Thomas Goodwin, together with four Scots—Robert Baillie, George Gillespie, Alexander Henderson, and Samuel Rutherford—was appointed to draft the Directory for the Public Worship of God. Actually, Young was the son of a Scottish manse, so the Scottish influence was considerable, and contributed to a directory whose structure was very like the Scottish Book of Common Order of 1564.[14]

Something of those closely involved may be noted. Thomas Goodwin and Philip Nye, whom Goodwin co-opted, were Independents opposed to a fixed liturgy, and the rest of the subcommittee were Presbyterians. Marshall, said to be the best preacher in England, was a Presbyterian, but anxious for accommodation. Herle was a definite Presbyterian, but very fair-minded, and often sided with the Independents in debate, while Gillespie and Rutherford were also very much against a prescribed liturgy,[15] Baillie and Henderson somewhat less so.

13. F. N. McCoy, *Robert Baillie and the Second Scots Reformation* (Berkeley: University of California Press, 1974), 90.
14. A point noted by Davies, *Worship*, 128. Note Alexander Henderson's description in his *The Government and Order of the Church of Scotland* (Edinburgh, 1841) in the unpaginated preface: "although they [ministers] be not tied to set forms and words, yet they are not left at random, but for testifying their consent and keeping unity, they have their directory and prescribed order."
15. Bryan D. Spinks, *Sacraments, Ceremonies and the Stuart Divines: Sacramental theology and liturgy in England and Scotland 1603–1662* (Aldershot: Ashgate, 2002), 120.

The first two-thirds of the directory, down to and including "Sanctification of the Lord's Day," was completed and signed November 20, 1644, and the balance progressively until December 27, 1644. It was passed by the House of Commons on January 3, 1645, and approved by both houses the following day. Thus the directory was the first completed production of the Assembly.

On January 23, 1645, Robert Baillie, one of the Scottish commissioners to the Assembly of Divines, addressed the Church of Scotland Assembly, in Edinburgh:

> That an Assembly and Parliament of England unanimously (which is their word) abolished, not only those ceremonies which troubled us, but the whole service-book, as a very idol (so speak they also) and a vessel full of much mischief; that in place of Episcopacy a Scots presbytery should be concluded in an English Assembly, and ordained in an English Parliament; as it is already ordained in the House of Commons, that the practice of the Church of Scotland, set down in a most wholesome, pious and prudent Directory, should come in place of a Liturgy in all the three dominions; such stories lately told, would have been counted fancies, dreams, merely impossibilities; yet this day we tell them as truths, and deeds done, for the great honour of our God, and, we are persuaded, the joy of many a godly soul. If any will not believe our report, let them trust their own eyes; for behold the warrant of our words, written and subscribed by the hands of the clerks of the Parliament of England, and the scribes of the Assembly there.[16]

On February 3 the Scottish Church adopted it with certain qualifications, and the Scottish Parliament ratified it three days later in the same terms, in both cases without a contrary voice.

The directory was published in London on March 18, 1645, with a few adjustments requested by the Scots, and an Ordinance of Parliament on April 17, 1645, replaced the Book of Common Prayer with the directory. Thereafter, the former no longer had legal stand-

16. Robert Baillie McCoy, 99.

ing, although use still occurred,[17] despite the hefty fines.[18] The legal status of the directory disappeared in England and Wales with the restoration of the monarchy and the royal assent to the Act of Uniformity, May 19, 1662. A modest revision of the Book of Common Prayer proposed at the Savoy Conference the previous year had been refused by the bishops. The implementation of the Act of Uniformity led to "the Great Ejection," when about 20 percent (approximately two thousand) of the English clergy resigned or were removed for refusing the requisite oath. The oath required, *inter alia*, an

> unfeigned assent and consent to all and everything contained and prescribed in and by the book entitled the Book of Common Prayer, and Administration of the Sacraments, and other Rites and Ceremonies of the Church, according to the use of the Church of England . . .

Only in the 1690s did the directory begin to have a wide use in the nonconformist churches in England, where "it was regarded as a key to recovering a simple, sincere, and unpretentious form of worship which was faithful to Scripture, and edifying for the congregation."[19]

In Scotland, Parliamentary sanction for the directory was repealed by the Act Rescissory of March 26, 1661. In 1662–63 perhaps 30 percent of ministers were deprived for refusing to conform to the new Episcopal order,[20] a high percentage given that there was no real

17. Spinks, *Sacraments*, 119; Anthony Fletcher in *Oliver Cromwell and the English Revolution*, ed. John Morrill (London: Longmans, 1990), 218; it seems likely that discreet use of the Anglican liturgy was overlooked. Christopher Durston, "By the book or with the spirit: the debate over liturgical prayer during the English Revolution," *Historical Research* 79 (2006): 50–73, emphasizes the variety of practice from 1645–60.

18. T. Leishman, *The Westminster Directory* (Edinburgh: William Blackwood, 1901), xix. *An Ordinance of the Lords and Commons Assembled in Parliament for the more effectual putting in execution The Directory For publique worship* . . . (August 23, 1645) required existing prayer books to be destroyed, and private or public use was prohibited. Penalties were severe: £5 for a first offense, £10 for a second, and prison for a year for a third. Opposition to the use of the directory or failure to observe it could result in a minister's being fined up to £50. Fines were to be used for poor relief.

19. Hughes Oliphant Old, *The Reading and Preaching of the Scriptures in the Worship of the Christian Church*, vol. 5 (Grand Rapids: Eerdmans, 2004), 28.

20. J. D. Douglas, *Light in the North* (Exeter: Paternoster Press, 1964), 100. Robert Woodrow (1679–1734) in his *The History of the Sufferings of the Church of Scotland* (Glasgow: Blackie

attempt to change the pattern of Scottish worship. Although Presbyterian church government and the Confession of Faith were restored in Scotland at the Revolution in 1690, the directory did not receive renewed civil sanction. However, the directory still continued to be the law of the Church of Scotland, and remains so to the present. Nevertheless, the Church of Scotland Assembly made reference to the directory only four times in the 250 years after its adoption—in 1694, 1705, 1736, and 1856.[21]

Of course, the directory was exported from Scotland with migration, but did not survive in its original form past 1789 in the major body of Presbyterians in the United States, although it managed to survive unaltered in the Covenanter Church there until 1945.[22] In Ireland it was modified, but not in essentials, by the Synod of Ulster in 1825 and subsequently.[23] In Australia it was discarded in the Basis of Union of 1901 forming the Presbyterian Church of Australia out of several state churches, and nothing took its place. It is retained in the Presbyterian Church of Eastern Australia.

Thus far the directory's origin and public history.

The Reasons for and General Nature of the Directory

Citing the manuscript minutes of the Assembly, Robert S. Paul writes:

> On May 24th, 1644, Stephen Marshall, as chairman of the committee responsible for this preliminary work, presented the general reasons

---

& Son, 1828) 1:324–29, provides lists with almost 400 names, equalling about 40 percent of the ministers. This would be the upper figure, and would include the bulk of the Protesters and a minority of the more moderate Resolutioners.

21. Leishmann, *Westminster Directory*, xxxi. In 1694 recovery of the custom of lecturing is urged, and in 1705 the "due observance" of the directory. In 1736 men are urged to "consider and observe the directory of this Church concerning the preaching of the Word," while in 1856 ministers are enjoined "to observe the recommendations contained in it respecting the reading of the Scriptures of the Old and New Testament at each diet of worship," and the hope is also expressed "that the principles maintained in that Directory will be duly observed."

22. J. A. Delivuk, *The Doctrine and History of Worship in the Reformed Presbyterian Church of North America* (Pittsburg, 1982), 126.

23. Robert Tosh, "Presbyterian Worship Through the Ages," *Bulletin of the Presbyterian Historical Society of Ireland* 28 (2001–3): 9.

for a Directory and the criteria employed by his committee—to find a mean between a completely fixed liturgy and a form of worship in which everyone would be "left to do his own will."[24]

This is confirmed from the preface that forms part of the directory. It is there acknowledged that the first reformers had removed much that "they then by the word, discovered to be vain, erroneous, superstitious, and idolatrous, in the Public Worship of God." But while the Book of Common Prayer provided for a service in the common tongue without the Mass, and for reading of the Scripture, "long and sad experience" had shown that the Church of England liturgy had ill effects. The "urging reading of all the prayers," "the many unprofitable and burdensome ceremonies contained in it," had caused difficulties. Good Christians had stayed away from the Lord's Table. Some faithful men were unable in good conscience to exercise their ministry, while prelates and their supporters made the liturgy so important as to hinder or even force out the preaching. Roman Catholics thought the Book of Common Prayer went a long way in their direction and so confirmed them in their "superstition and idolatry," while the effect of the liturgy had been to further "an idle and unedifying ministry, which contented itself with set forms."

The preface affirms that love of novelty or intention to disparage the first Reformers was not the motivation for further reformation. Rather, further reformation was necessary to satisfy consciences, answer the expectation of other Reformed churches, answer the desires of many of the godly in Britain, and evidence the commitment to uniformity of public worship promised in the Solemn League and Covenant. "We have, after earnest and frequent calling upon the name of God, and after much consultation, not with flesh and blood but with his holy word, resolved to lay aside the former Liturgy, with the many rites and ceremonies formerly used in the worship of God; and have agreed upon this following Directory for all the parts of Public Worship, at ordinary and extraordinary times."

What is in the preface should be noted, and also what is not there. It is clearly not intended as a fixed liturgy as some in the Assembly desired,

24. Paul, *The Assembly of the Lord,* 364.

to whom Baillie refers, but neither does it condemn the English Book of Common Prayer outright, as the Scots wished.[25] Like many things about the Assembly, it represents a compromise. Indeed, as Marshall put it:

> This doth not only set down the heads of things but so largely as that with the altering of here and there a word, a man may mould it into a prayer.[26]

Marshall and his friends thought set prayers suited to exceptional cases such as new or ill-trained ministers, or lack of ministers. On May 16, 1645, a pamphlet of sixteen pages was published "by authority" in London entitled: *A supply of prayer for the ships of this kingdom that want ministers to pray with them: agreeable to the directory established by Parliament*[27] in which the approach noted by Marshall was taken, although this was not the normal intention.[28] So the directory was not against all set forms of prayer—it even recommends the use of the Lord's Prayer—but it was against requiring such. In this respect it was not dissimilar to the old familiar Book of Common Order from Knox's time. The only real difference was that it did not provide specimen prayers.[29]

The uniformity that the directory aimed for was, to use George Gillespie's words, "a uniformity in one and the same kind of things,"[30] all founded on Scripture. The preface itself put it this way:

25. Ibid., 392.

26. Ibid. The spelling has been modernized.

27. British Library copy. UMI Collection, reel number 47: E.284[16]. Attention was drawn to this point by Dr. Henry Hammond, chaplain to the king, in his *A View of the New Directory and a Vindication of the Ancient Liturgy of the Church of England* (Oxford, August 1645), 101ff. *A supply of prayer* is printed in Leishmann, *Westminster Directory*, 172–87; note his interesting comments on pages xix–xxi.

28. Compare B. B. Warfield's comment (*The Westminster Assembly and Its Work* [Grand Rapids: Baker, 1981], 45–46): "As is indicated by the title, the book is not 'a straight liturgy,' but a body of agenda and paradigms. Some of these paradigms, to be sure, are so full that they are capable of being transmuted into liturgical forms by a mere transposition of their clauses into the mode of direct address, but they were not intended to be so employed, and are too compressed to lend themselves readily to such use."

29. Thus the statement of R. J. Gore, in his *Covenantal Worship* (Phillipsburg, NJ: P&R, 2002), 44, that "allowance was made for the Scottish church to continue to use either its hallowed Knoxian Book of Common Order or the newer Directory" is not quite right. The new directory was alone prescribed, but it enabled a similar structure and type of service to Knox's liturgy.

30. *A Treatise of Miscellany Questions* ([1649] repr. Edinburgh, 1844), 84.

Our meaning being only that the general heads, the sense and scope of the prayers and other parts of Public Worship being known to all, there may be a consent of all the churches, in those things that contain the substance of the service and worship of God; and the ministers may be hereby directed in their administration to keep like soundness in doctrine and prayer; and may, if need be, have some help and furniture . . .

So we may say that the directory, by providing an outline of how worship should be conducted, offers a middle way between a fixed liturgy and leaving a minister entirely to his own devices. The directory is not always clear. As Van Dixhoorn notes, sometimes the directory says a minister *may* do something, and in other places it says he *shall*. Practices are variously termed "necessary" or "requisite," but also "expedient," "convenient," or "sufficient."[31] Still, these ambiguities, if we may call them that, are studied ambiguities, leaving room for supplementary regulation according to local circumstances. In the case of the Scottish Church the directory was approved without a dissenting voice on February 3, 1645, with the requirement that "according to the plain tenor and meaning thereof, and the intent of the Preface, it be carefully and uniformly observed and practised by all the ministers and others within this kingdom whom it doth concern." Four days later, the Assembly approved and adopted the report of its committee "for keeping the greater uniformity in this Kirk, in the practice and observations of the Directory in some points of public worship." This report shows that a general uniformity in matters of sacramental practice and in reading and expounding Scripture was desired by the Assembly.[32]

The Chief Principle in the Production of the Directory

After the preface comes the heading "A Directory for Public Prayer, Reading the Holy Scriptures, Singing of Psalms, Preaching

31. Chad B. Van Dixhoorn, *A Puritan Theology of Preaching* (St. Antholin's Lectureship Charity Lecture, London 2005), 12.
32. The text of the Act of Assembly February 7, 1645, is conveniently found in Leishman, *Westminster Directory*, 165–69. For a valuable article, "Presbyterian Liturgies," see Charles Hodge, *The Church and Its Polity* (London: Thomas Nelson & Sons, 1879), 157–67.

of the Word, Administration of the Sacraments, and other parts of the Public Worship of God, Ordinary and Extraordinary." The preface states that the concern has been "to hold forth such things as are of Divine institution in every Ordinance; and other things we have endeavoured to set forth according to the rules of Christian prudence, agreeable to the general rules of the word of God." This statement of what is commonly called "the regulative principle of worship" [RPW] is also set out in the Confession of Faith, which reached finality about two years after the Directory:

> **1.6:** "The whole counsel of God concerning all things necessary for his own glory, man's salvation, faith and life, is either expressly set down in scripture, or by good and necessary consequence may be deduced from Scripture: unto which nothing at any time is to be added . . . Nevertheless, . . . there are some circumstances concerning the worship of God, and government of the Church, common to human actions and societies, which are to be ordered by the light of nature and Christian prudence, according to the general rules of the word, which are always to be observed."[33]

The words "Divine institution in each Ordinance" refer to the several sections of the directory dealing with the elements of worship, and "other things" includes what is called by the confession "circumstances." I doubt that many English Protestants would have taken exception to this statement in the confession, except for Baptists. They changed "or by good and necessary consequence may be deduced from Scripture" to read "or necessarily contained in the Holy Scripture."[34]

Two further statements in the confession are relevant:

In **20.2** we read: "God alone is Lord of the conscience and hath left it free from the doctrines and commandments of men, which

33. Citations of the Westminster Confession are from the critical text in S. W. Carruthers, *The Westminster Confession of Faith* (Manchester: R. Aikman, 1937).

34. I doubt this was intended to be precisely equivalent contra S. E. Waldron, *A Modern Exposition of the 1689 Confession of Faith* (Darlington: Evangelical Press, 1989), 42–43. The corresponding texts of the Savoy Declaration of 1658 and the Baptist Confession of 1677/1689 are otherwise identical to the Westminster Confession. Baptists were sensitive about admitting "good and necessary consequence" lest they had to admit infant baptism. Cf. a more recent treatment in Fred Malone, *The Baptism of Disciples Alone* (Cape Coral, FL: Founders Press, 2003), 20–22.

are in any thing contrary to his word; or beside it, if matters of faith or worship."

This statement forbids matters of faith or worship additional to Scripture, and not just matters contrary to Scripture.

Finally, **21.1:** "But the acceptable way of worshipping the true God is instituted by himself, and so limited by his own revealed will, that he may not be worshipped according to the imaginations or devices of men, or the suggestions of Satan, under any visible representation, or any other way not prescribed in holy scripture."

This clause in the confession would create a difficulty for those who doted on ceremonies, symbolic vestments, and the like, and of course those who utilized "holy pictures."

Calvin and Westminster

Now let us compare these positions of the Westminster Assembly with the teaching of John Calvin, for it is often claimed that the Westminster men are at considerable variance with him.[35] For contrast, let me first state a word or two about Luther's position.

For Luther the tight regulation of worship in the Old Testament law given to the Jews was contrasted with the more liberal position under the gospel. Indeed, the first commandment as understood by Luther (embracing our common first and second) was seen (1) as

35. I do not think J. I. Packer is correct in stating that "the idea that direct biblical warrant, in the form of precept or precedent, is required to sanction every substantive item included in the public worship of God was in fact a Puritan innovation." *Among God's Giants*, 326. It depends on what is meant by "substantive"—a word omitted in the original lecture in 1963—but the statement is in any case too broad. Similarly, Iain Murray in *To Glorfy and Enjoy God*, ed. J.W. Carson and D.W. Hall (Edinburgh: Banner of Truth, 1994), 176–78, is too general in his discussion of the RPW. The discussion by Douglas Kelly, "The Puritan Regulative Principle and Contemporary Worship," in J. L. Duncan, *The Westminster Confession into the 21st Century*, vol. 2 (Fearn: Mentor, 2004), 67ff., also needs to be more carefully nuanced, particularly to distinguish the main body of Puritans from the narrower Independents, and similarly R. J. Gore, *Covenantal Worship*, while Jeffrey J. Meyers, *The Lord's Service* (Moscow, ID: Canon Press, 2003), 303, confuses elements and forms. I forbear to mention those writers not friendly to Reformed theology.

prohibiting an image one worships, not images as such, and (2) as superseded under the gospel to the extent that images may be useful teaching aids and will not hurt any who do not have an idol in their heart already. Unless they are grossly bound up with corruption of the fundamentals of the gospel, there is no need to destroy them.

This was Luther's argument against the iconoclasm of Karlstadt in the mid-1520s.[36] His basic principle was similar to that of the Roman Catholics,[37] only the application was different, given Luther's grasp of the true doctrine of salvation by grace through faith. Thus, practices repugnant to justification by faith apart from works were excluded from worship, but others allowed.

Calvin's thought was somewhat different. In his *Form of Administering Baptism* (1542), Calvin adds this note:

We know that elsewhere there are many other ceremonies which we deny not to be very ancient, but because they have been invented at pleasure, or at least on grounds which, be these what they may, must be trivial, since they have been devised without authority from the word of God, and because, on the other hand, so many superstitions have sprung from them, we have felt no hesitation in abolishing them, in order that there might be nothing to prevent the people from going directly to Jesus Christ. First, whatever is not commanded, we are not free to choose. Secondly, nothing which does not tend to edification ought to be received into the Church. If anything of the kind has been introduced, it ought to be taken away, and by much stronger reason, whatever tends only to cause scandal, and

36. Carlo M. N. Eire, *War Against the Idols: The Reformation of Worship from Erasmus to Calvin* (Cambridge: Cambridge University Press, 1986), 65–73.
37. Note the 1994 *Catechism of the Catholic Church* 2129–132: "The divine injunction included the prohibition of every representation by the hand of man . . . Nevertheless, already in the Old Testament, God ordained or permitted the making of images that pointed symbolically toward salvation by the incarnate Word: so it was with the bronze serpent, the ark of the covenant, and the cherubim. Basing itself on the mystery of the incarnate Word, the seventh ecumenical council at Nicaea (787) justified against the iconoclasts the veneration of icons—of Christ, but also of the Mother of God, the angels, and all the saints. By becoming incarnate, the Son of God introduced a new 'economy' of images. The Christian veneration of images is not contrary to the first commandment which proscribes idols. Indeed, 'the honour rendered to an image passes to its prototype,' and 'whoever venerates an image venerates the person portrayed in it.' The honour paid to sacred images is a 'respectful veneration,' not the adoration due to God alone."

is, as it were, an instrument of idolatry and false opinion, ought on no account to be tolerated.[38]

While we could play semantic games with what is meant by "commanded" by Scripture—obviously Luther thought his approach was scriptural—there is no denying the fact that Calvin operated on a more radical principle than Luther. For Calvin, it was impossible to suppose that in the context of worship an image or picture of Christ was without theological significance. He writes:

> Again, to what end do the Papists set up images in Churches? Is it to have knowledge of their histories? No: but there stands a sort of puppets with demure countenances, as it were to summon folk to do them homage, insomuch that an image is not so soon set up in a Church, but by and by folk go and kneel down to it and do a kind of worship to it. And can a man devise to tear the majesty of our Lord Jesus Christ, and to deface his glory more, than by the things that the Papists do? Behold, they paint and portray Jesus Christ, who (as we know) is not only man, but also God manifested in the flesh: and what a representation is that? . . . Is it not a wiping away of that which is chiefest in our Lord Jesus Christ, that is to wit, of his divine majesty?[39]

John H. Leith is right to affirm that "Calvin's application of the second commandment, 'Thou shalt not make any graven image,' eliminated the visual arts from the worship and meditative life of the church."[40] Calvin's viewpoint was pervasive in the Reformed church, providing quite a contrast to Lutheran practice. Calvinists were opposed to images and pictures, and cautious about ceremonies.

We can summarize Calvin's teaching on worship as follows:

38. Henry Beveridge, ed., *Selected Works of John Calvin* (Grand Rapids: Baker, 1983), 2:117–18.

39. *Sermons on Deuteronomy* [1555–56], trans. Arthur Golding (London, 1583; repr. Banner of Truth, 1987), serm. 23, 138; cf. serm. 82, 504.

40. John H. Leith, *An Introduction to the Reformed Tradition* (Atlanta: John Knox Press, 1977), 166. Calvin expressly condemns pictures of Christ in the church. See further Hughes Oliphant Old, "Calvin's Theology of Worship," in *Give Praise to God*, ed. P. G. Ryken, D. W. H. Thomas, and J. L. Duncan, (Phillipsburg, NJ: P&R Publishing, 2003), 412–35.

1. In the *Form for Baptism*: "First, whatever is not commanded, we are not free to choose."[41] In the *Institutes*: "God wills to be worshipped as he commands and we are not to mingle inventions of our own."[42] In his *sermons*: "But we are to follow in all simplicity what he has ordained by his Word, without adding anything to it at all. For as soon as we fall away from that, however slightly, whatever case we might cite, and try to justify ourselves, God will surely punish us."[43]

2. "Secondly, nothing which does not tend to edification ought to be received into the Church. If anything of the kind has been introduced, it ought to be taken away, and by much stronger reason, whatever tends only to cause scandal, and is, as it were, an instrument of idolatry and false opinion, ought on no account to be tolerated."[44]

The distinction between these two points is broadly that refers (1) to elements or parts of worship, and (2) to the form and rubrics of worship that enable worship to be expressed in a particular setting. The form of worship includes the way of doing a particular thing. Thus, prayer is an element of worship, the Lord's Prayer is a form of prayer, and a rubric would be an instruction whether to stand, sit, or kneel. Circumstances such as time, place, type of seating—the non religious aspects "common to human actions and societies"—are not mentioned since, one might imagine, Calvin took such things as self-evident.[45] The form and rubrics are within the authority of the church, subject to scriptural requirements, particularly the demand of edification.

41. *Form of Administering Baptism*, 1542 (see especially footnote 28).
42. *Institutes* (ed. Battles), 4.10.23.
43. B. W. Farley, trans. & ed., *John Calvin's Sermons on the Ten Commandments* (Grand Rapids: Baker, 1980), 66.
44. *Form of Administering Baptism*, 1542 (see especially footnote 33).
45. I have profited from the distinction between element, form, rubric, and circumstance in T. David Gordon's review entitled "The Westminster Assembly's Unworkable and Unscriptural View of Worship," *Westminster Theological Journal* 65 (2003): 345–56, of R. J. Gore's work *Covenantal Worship* (Phillipsburg, NJ: P&R Publishing, 2002). Although I think Gordon is essentially correct in his analysis, I have not found the subject presented in quite such a fashion in the original literature, and this may account for the lack of documentation in Gordon's article. On this aspect Gore's strictures in "Covenantal Worship: Reconsidering the Critics," *Westminster Theological Journal* 67 (2005): 367ff., are to the point.

It has been claimed by Charles Baird that Calvin highly approved set forms of prayer from which ministers should not be allowed to vary. Baird offered the following translation from Calvin's Latin letter of 1548 to Lord Somerset:

> As to what concerns a form of prayer and ecclesiastical rites, I highly approve of it that there be a certain form, from which the ministers be not allowed to vary: That first, some provision be made to help the simplicity and unskilfulness of some; secondly, that the consent and harmony of the churches one with another may appear; and lastly, that the capricious giddiness and levity of such as affect innovations may be prevented. To which end I have showed that a Catechism will be very useful. Therefore there ought to be a stated Catechism, a stated form of prayer, and administration of the sacraments.[46]

However, the standard English translation made in 1858 (shortly after Baird wrote) indicates the reference is to the importance of a set catechism, *not* to a form of prayers. Indeed, the point he is dealing with is "the sound instruction of the people," and he considers that as well as vital preaching there should be "an explicit summary of the doctrine which all ought to preach" and a common formula of instruction for little children or ignorant persons.

> Indeed, I do not say that it may not be well, and even necessary, to bind down the pastors and curates to a certain written form, as well for the sake of supplementing the ignorance and deficiencies of some, as the better to manifest the conformity and agreement between all the churches; thirdly, to take away all ground of pretence for bringing in any eccentricity or new fangled doctrine on the part of those who only seek to indulge an idle fancy; as I have already said, the catechism ought to serve as a check upon such people.

46. Baird, *Presbyterian Liturgies*, 23, who has been followed by too many who partially cite Baird's purported quotation of Calvin in a context of prayer rather than catechesis, e.g., D. G. Hart in his *Recovering Mother Kirk* (Grand Rapids: Baker, 2003), 26. Similarly, W. D. Maxwell, *A History of Worship in the Church of Scotland* (London: Oxford University Press, 1955), 72–73, a standard but not always accurate writer, who purports to cite Calvin's Latin *Opera*, but his citation is in identical words to Baird's translation. Baird also refers to Bingham's *Antiquities*, but the reference he gives [2:747] is not relevant to the issue. Perhaps Baird worked from imperfect notes brought back from his period of study in Europe.

He immediately adds:

> There is besides, the form and manner of administration of the sacraments; also the public prayers. But whatever, in the meantime, be the arrangement in regard to these matters, care must be taken not to quench the efficacy which ought to attend the preaching of the Gospel.[47]

We know Calvin used a set liturgy in the Sunday worship, although there was some freedom on the weekdays,[48] and "discretion" in the prayer for illumination on Sunday.[49] The reasons noted by him about the importance of a catechism may well have influenced him in regard to set prayers, but he also approved of Knox's "discretionary liturgy," and we know of his unwillingness to insist on uniformity in such matters. Indeed, Hughes Oliphant Old is to the point when he writes of Calvin:

> He published forms of prayer for his congregation. He developed the gift of extempore prayer in the daily prayer services of Geneva, but he knew that prayer was much more than a form of prayer or an ability to extemporize public prayer. Prayer was for him the principal exercise of religion . . . The liturgist of today who would listen to

47. Jules Bonnet, ed., *Selected Works of John Calvin* ([1858] Grand Rapids: Baker, 1983), 5:191–92.

48. Cf. "In the working days the preacher maketh such exhortation unto prayer, as seemeth unto himself most meet: applying or framing the same, both to the time and matter which he entreateth of in his sermon. The Sunday morning, immediately before the sermon, the preacher useth commonly a manner of prayer, as hereafter followeth . . . The rest to be said in the weekday, of prayer, is set out before in the second side of the fourth leaf, among the prayers for Sunday . . ." *The forme of common prayers used in the churches of Geneva*, translated from the French by William Huycke (London 1550), fol. i, fol. xxiii.

49. It is commonly said that there was a "set" prayer at this point as by T. H. L. Parker, *John Calvin* (Tring: Lion Publishing, 1982), 103. However, note the following: "When the preacher hath on this wise made his supplication, the whole multitude singeth some Psalm in plainsong (the which thing done) the preacher beginneth to make his prayer again, that God of his grace would vouchsafe to send down his Holy Spirit, as well that he may set forth the word to the advancement of God's honour and edifying of the people: as that the hearers may also receive it humbly with obedience due unto the same. *The manner of prayer is referred to the discretion of the preacher.* Immediately after the sermon, when the preacher hath exhorted the people to pray, he beginneth on this wise: . . ." *The forme . . .*, fol. iii (emphasis supplied). The provision for an extemporaneous prayer for illumination derives from Calvin's period in Strasburg 1537–41, and his adoption of Bucer's liturgy.

Calvin must be prepared to go beyond questions of liturgical rites and forms. These formal problems must be solved, to be sure, but deeper spiritual problems must be solved at the same time. For Calvin, worship is the sanctifying work of God's Spirit in the hearts of his people.[50]

If the English liturgy had been free of objectionable ceremonies, many of the godly would probably have been content with the set prayers, for the mainstream opinion certainly did not hold that set prayers were in principle objectionable. At any rate, there does not appear to be any substantial difference between Calvin and the seventeenth-century English Puritans, if one excepts the more radical Independents.[51] For Calvin, the ceremonies that were not otherwise unlawful biblically were indifferent things. The thirty-fourth Article of the Church of England (1563) need not of itself be objectionable, although it became so. It reads:

> It is not necessary that traditions and ceremonies be in all places one, or utterly like, for at all times they have been diverse, and may be changed according to the diversity of countries, times and men's manners, so that nothing be ordained against God's word.
>
> Whosoever through his private judgement, willingly and purposely doth openly break the traditions and ceremonies of the church, which be not repugnant to the word of God, and be ordained and approved by common authority, ought to be rebuked openly (that others may fear to do the like), as he that offendeth against the Common order of the Church and hurteth the authority of the Magistrate, and woundeth the conscience of the weak brethren.
>
> Every particular or national Church hath authority to ordain, change, and abolish ceremonies or rites of the Church ordained only by man's authority, so that all things be done to edifying.

50. Old, "Calvin's Theology of Worship," 435.

51. The Independents objected on principle to any prescribed prayers, John Owen going so far as to regard congregational use of the Lord's Prayer as unlawful in the context of his 1655 book against the anti-Trinitarian John Biddle (*Vindiciae Evangelicae*, ch. 34 *The Works of John Owen* [Goold ed.], vol. 12, esp. 577–79), although his chief objection seems to have been against *imposed* prayers/liturgy (*Discourse concerning Liturgies* [1662], *Works*, vol. 15, esp. 21). While the agenda of the Independents was not achieved at the Westminster Assembly, their influence on Presbyterians subsequently has been significant.

Although he would not think it expedient to comply with sticklers for every point, and though in the Anglican liturgy, as it was described to him by the English exiles at Frankfurt, "there were many silly things that might be tolerated," Calvin counseled a prudent endeavor to "compose anew the form that will seem best adapted for the use and edification" of the church in Frankfurt.[52] These words, written in 1555, agree with his words to Lord Somerset in 1548 in which, while urging conformity to the Word of God, Calvin states:

I willingly acknowledge that we must observe moderation, and that overdoing is neither discreet or useful; indeed, that forms of worship need to be accommodated to the condition and tastes of the people. But the corruptions of Satan and of Antichrist must not be admitted under that pretext.[53]

To similar effect is his letter to the church at Wenzel in 1554 where he stresses to the recipients, who were private individuals and not pastors, that one should accommodate oneself to the use of ceremonies where they are established and when one has no authority to oppose them. [He refers to lighted candles and figured bread in the Eucharist.]

In this counsel Calvin sounds very much like a person in a church with the Thirty-nine Articles. Calvin goes on to state:

If we were called upon to receive such ceremonies, we should hold ourselves bound to the position in which God hath placed us, to admit of no compromise in resisting their introduction, and in maintaining constantly the purity which the church confided to us already possesses.

This sounds like the approach at the Westminster Assembly where reform was officially on the agenda and one has the authority to bring about change.

Calvin adds:

52. J. Bonnet, ed., *Selected Works of John Calvin*, 7 vols. (Grand Rapids: Baker, 1983), 6: 118; cf. the letter to John Knox in the same volume, 189–91.
53. Ibid., 5:193.

But should our lot be cast in some place where a different form prevails, there is not one of us who from spite against a candle or a chasuble [outer cloak/vestment] would consent to separate himself from the body of the church, and so deprive himself of the use of the sacrament . . . It would be for us matter of deep regret, if the French church that might be erected there [in Wenzel] should be broken up, because we would not accommodate ourselves to some ceremonies which do not affect the substance of the faith. For as we have said, it is perfectly lawful for the children of God to submit themselves to many things of which they do not approve. Now the main point of consideration is, how far such liberty should extend. Upon this head, let us lay it down as a settled point, that we ought to make mutual concessions in all ceremonies, that do not involve any prejudice to the confession of our faith, and for this end that the unity of the church be not destroyed by our excessive rigour or moroseness.[54]

This sounds like the approach of the main body of Puritans in the agitation for reforms in the 1570s and later. It is also seen in the way in which many good men conformed to the state of things established following the restoration of the monarchy in 1660.

I am quite satisfied there is no fundamental difference between Calvin and the Westminster men on worship. They are in agreement in the principle, and the differences in form and rubric are those which a church, in due subjection to Scripture, may maintain without schism. Both, when it is possible, remove all doubtful religious ceremonies, or those that have become a snare. Both are keenly concerned for the unity of the church, and will strive to accommodate to maintain that unity.

The Definition of "Circumstances"

A further note on the circumstances of worship is appropriate. When we look at the position among the Puritans (and others) in the period before the Westminster Assembly, we find that many defended the liturgy using the argument that the ceremonies were not worship

---

54. *Selected Works of John Calvin*, 6:30–31.

as such but adjuncts to worship, or legitimate applications of worship not requiring specific authorization. John Burges (1563–1635) writes in 1631:

> Whatever therefore is ordained in the church, as an *Arbitrary* and *moveable* Rite or Ceremony, in the use whereof no *Immediate* or proper worship of God is placed, but the thing in itself still reckoned indifferent; that is a matter of *mere Order, sensu largo*, in the large acceptation of *Order*.[55]

John Ball (1585–1640), usually reckoned as one of the fathers of English Presbyterianism, just before his death in 1640 writes against separatists who rejected a set liturgy or read prayers:

> No man has authority to devise any substantial means of worship, which must be referred to the second commandment, no more than he may teach new doctrines or institute new sacraments in God's church upon his own head. But the order, phrase or method, which is devised by man, is no worship of God.[56]

Therefore Ball insists that

> a stinted [fixed] public form of prayer is the breach of no commandment, no forbidden invention of man, either in the deviser or the user, in the case of necessity or otherwise.[57]

Laurence Womock (1612–86), later bishop of St. Davids, defended the liturgy and episcopacy. He refers to Calvin and Beza's stress on the lawful authority of the church, and adds that the strict Presbyterians (he cites Smectymnuus) acknowledge that

> many conscientious men have conformed to ceremonies on this ground as supposing that Authority did not make them matters of

---

55. John Burges, *The Lawfulness of Kneeling in the Act of Receiving the Lord's Supper* (London, 1631), 10. Burges had resigned over the surplice question about 1591, opposed the 1603 canons, and been ejected, but became rector of Sutton Coldfield in 1617.

56. John Ball, *A Friendly Triall of the Grounds Tending to Separation* (Cambridge, 1640), 49.

57. Ibid., 53.

worship but of ordered decency; and thus they satisfied their consciences in answering those texts, Col 2:20–22; Matt 15:9.[58]

But the controversy from the 1630s onward ultimately led to stricter Presbyterians, more clearly distinguishing "circumstances common to human actions and societies" from "other things" or "circumstances" of distinctly religious character, that is, ceremonies strictly taken. These were rejected, although forms and rubrics necessarily remained to enable worship to be expressed in an edifying manner.
George Gillespie writes in 1637:

The church of Christ being a society of men and women, must either observe order and decency in all the circumstances of their holy actions, time, place, person, form, etc., or else be deformed with that disorder and confusion which common reason and civility abhors. Ceremonies, therefore, which are sacred observances, and serve only a religious and holy use, and which may not, without sacrilege, be applied to another use, must be sorted with things of another nature than circumstances.[59]

So there is something of a refinement of argument to eliminate religious ceremonies that are not genuine "circumstances" common to human actions and societies. This does not end all discussion since people differed in smaller matters on how to apply this distinction in practice.[60] Older conservative Scots like Baillie had no problem with using the Apostles' Creed or the Doxology, but these

58. Laurence Womock, *Beaten Oyle for the Lamps of the Sanctuarie* (London, 1641), 52.
59. George Gillespie, *A Dispute Against English Popish Ceremonies obtruded on the Church of Scotland* ([Leiden, 1637] repr. Edinburgh, 1844), 130. Note also W. D. J. McKay, *An Ecclesiastical Republic: Church Government in the Writings of George Gillespie* (Carlisle: Paternoster, 1997), 92–96.
60. Gore acknowledges (*Covenantal Worship*) that exactly the same problem of "disagreement on the appropriate application" (142) exists if we adopt his "covenantal worship" proposal, which includes the traditional RPW plus "whatever is consistent with the Scriptures" (139–40). His proposal would allow "movement, posture, music, drama, art, and the wise use of sacred space and sacred time" (156), otherwise described as *adiaphora* or things indifferent, although these things extra to the RPW "must not be imposed and made mandatory" (147). Gore is right to speak of worship as simple, orderly, free, worship that glorifies and edifies, that is catholic, culturally sensitive, balanced, and Christ-centered (143–61), but it is not altogether easy to see that his "covenantal worship" theory sufficiently anchors worship to the biblical pattern, which, of course, is not a uniformity of words but of things, thus allowing for a certain diversity.

were not mentioned in the directory in deference to an element of narrower opinion.

Conclusion

I have sought to illustrate the directory's character as an authoritative guide to Christian worship based on a carefully nuanced understanding of the regulative principle of worship in essential continuity with John Calvin. It is also in continuity with Calvin in its concern for the spirituality of worship, hence its emphasis on the Word of God and prayer. "For Calvin there was no liturgical reform without teaching people to pray. The liturgist of today who would listen to Calvin must go beyond questions of liturgical rites and forms . . . They must aspire above all to glorify God in spirit and in truth."[61] The directory can do much to help us in this endeavor.

Gore's position seems to be formulated too much against a rather confined view of the RPW so as to move somewhat to another extreme.

61. Old, "Calvin's Theology of Worship," 435.

6

Elements and Practice[1]

I have previously demonstrated the aim of the Directory for Public Worship as an outline of worship rather than as a fixed liturgy, and that it is controlled by the application of the regulative principle. (Perhaps, if we recall our Savior's words requiring that we teach whatever he has commanded, we might speak of the regulative *principal*.)

The directory is slightly longer than the Westminster Confession of Faith. It runs to a little over 12,600 words, including the preface. Perhaps this is a reminder that it is not simply an outline of how worship may be conducted, but a handbook of pastoral practice as well.

The chapter headings of the directory illustrate this:

Of the Assembling of the Congregation, and their Behaviour in the Public Worship of God
Of Public Reading of the Holy Scriptures
Of Public Prayer before the Sermon
Of the Preaching of the Word
Of Prayer after Sermon
Of the Administration of the Sacraments: and First of Baptism
Of the Celebration of the Communion, or the Sacrament of the Lord's Supper
Of the Sanctification of the Lord's Day
The Solemnization of Marriage

1. An expanded version of a lecture given at Westminster Theological Seminary, Philadelphia, on October 22, 2004, on the occasion of the seventy-fifth anniversary of the seminary.

Concerning Visiting the Sick
Concerning Burial of the Dead
Concerning Public Solemn Fasting
Of Singing of Psalms
APPENDIX: Touching Days and Places for Public Worship

Text

Before considering the content of the directory, let me give a word about the text of the document. Manuscript copies of the directory were located in 2002,[2] and in comparing them with the printed text, the changes that occurred between the signed "advice" of the Assembly to Parliament and the final document are evident. These are chiefly the inclusion of the last paragraph in the section concerning reading of the Scriptures, omission of specified questions at baptism, abbreviation of the qualifications for admission to the Lord's Supper, the understandable omission of a recommendation for a law regulating consent in marriage, and revision in the section on visiting the sick. Additionally, what Chris Coldwell says of the general printing practice of the time is true of the directory. Coldwell writes:

> The printing shop in the early stages of the hand press became responsible for standardizing capitalization, use of italics, spelling and punctuation—the "incidentals" of the text as opposed to the "substantials" such as the words themselves.[3]

Thus the printed text shows many variations from the manuscript in these matters, despite the care the Assembly took in printing their productions. There is no reason to suppose that the scribes of the Assembly did not review the printer's proofs and so could correct any objectionable changes in the "incidentals." Nevertheless, the customary freedom given printers in the incidentals should caution against ill-founded conclusions such as that *Psalms* with a capital *P* means

---

2. Refer Bibliography 1.1 in C. Van Dixhoorn, "Reforming the Reformation: Theological Debate at the Westminster Assembly, 1643–1652" (PhD diss., 7 vols., University of Cambridge, 2004).

3. "Examining the Work of S. W. Carruthers," *The Confessional Presbyterian* 1 (2005): 45.

the Psalter, but *psalms* with a lowercase *p* means a religious song of a more general nature, or that *publick* spelled with a *c-k* is the original (in fact it was *publique* spelled with a *q-u-e*).[4]

Content Overview

Coming now to the actual content of the directory, it is to be noted that it does not introduce the subject of worship by a general summary statement such as prefaces the Assembly's next production, the *Form of Church Government*. It would have been very helpful if the Assembly had described worship explicitly in terms of a meeting of the triune God and his covenant people. This was their unchallenged assumption, but they did not see fit to outline it as such in a practical document such as the directory, and we are left to glean it from scattered references. The gleaning is not difficult. Using its own language, we may say that the directory considers worship to involve appearing in a special way before the incomparably great and majestic Lord, in the name and mediation of Jesus Christ, through whose blood we have remission of sin, that we may have fellowship with God. All this is through the Spirit of grace and adoption, who sanctifies us so that we may have the life of God in Christ and grace to enable for every duty to God and humanity.

In chapter 21 of the confession, written in 1646, a very nice balance of statement concerning the elements of worship appears that

---

4. We now have the manuscript text of the directory that the Assembly retained as its own copy ("the Assembly's copy"). The repeated use of "R" in the margin against each paragraph presumably indicates "Resolved," while the alterations made subsequently by Parliament have been made by insertion and/or deletion. There are also small notations in the margin at two points, which indicates some involvement of the printer. Thus there is a "25" and a "31" with flourishes (perhaps signature marks "F" and "G," respectively) against the points at which an eight-page signature begins, equating to pages 33 [F] and 41 [G] in the first printed edition (which included eight pages for the preface before the beginning of the directory proper). A square bracket in the text equating to the beginning of signature I (page 57) is also found. The copy submitted by the Assembly to the House of Commons is lost, and the copy submitted to the House of Lords has no such changes or marks, nor, of course, has the vellum copy of the Parliament-approved text made by the Lords. I assume the Assembly's copy, with its annotations and corrections, was used in some way in preparing the printed copy. I have had access to the Assembly's copy and the copy made for the Lords through the kindness of Dr. Chad Van Dixhoorn, Cambridge, and I have discussed the issues with Mr. Chris Coldwell of Naphtali Press—cf. *The Confessional Presbyterian* 1 (2005): app. D, 61–62.

indicates both the item and the manner in which it is to be done. The ordinary elements mentioned there are prayer, reading of Scripture, preaching of the Word, singing, and the use of the sacraments, with fast or thanksgiving days on occasion. The directory covered these items, but also included guidance in regard to weddings and visiting the sick because they were embraced in the earlier books that the directory was to replace; and fasting was in the Scottish book and burial in the English one.[5] The directory's extensive prayer outlines (over a quarter of the content) and lengthy section on visiting the sick remind us of its pastoral emphasis.

Offering

The customary giving for the relief of the poor at the close of communion is mentioned in the Directory, as also on days of public thanksgiving and public humiliation; but in neither the directory nor the confession is an offering otherwise referred to. This reflects the practice of that age in maintaining the church ministry, services, and buildings from the public purse. In some British settings, as well as in America, the offering of the people not only for the poor but for general church purposes early assumed a larger role in the absence of endowment by the state.[6] The directory urges that the collection for the poor not hinder the worship. An act of the Church of Scotland Assembly in 1648 actually forbade the collection during the service as "a very great and unseemly disturbance of Divine Worship."[7] With large congregations and few fixed pews, one can understand this.

Length of Service

The directory insists that the service and all its parts should be so conducted as to provide appropriate balance—no parts being

5. Iain H. Murray, in *To Glorify and Enjoy God*, John L. Carson and David W. Hall, ed., (Edinburgh: Banner of Truth, 1994), 174.
6. In Scotland, those who seceded from the Established Church in 1733 are an early example of voluntary support. Cf. also John H. Leith, *An Introduction to the Reformed Tradition* (Atlanta: John Knox Press, 1977), 185.
7. W. M. McMillan, *The Worship of the Scottish Reformed Church 1560–1638* (London: James Clarke & Co., 1931), 123. Collection at the church door had long been customary although obviously not universal in the 1640s.

unduly restricted or rendered tedious. The great English Puritan Thomas Cartwright (1535–1603) considered the ordinary Anglican service (without communion) excessive in length at around two hours. He thought that the readings and prayers crowded out preaching. "Through such continuance the powers of the mind standing so long bent are dulled, and often also a most dangerous loathsomeness occasioned." Accordingly, the ordinary service (without communion) should be about one hour and a half, allowing an hour for preaching.[8] Even the communion preliminary should be a "brief exhortation" closed by "a few words." If leaders in the 1580s thought 90 minutes a suitable time limit, sixty years later 150 minutes was not unusual for the ordinary service.[9] In part this was due to the common later Puritan practice of providing a twenty- to thirty-minute exposition of the Scripture reading—a practice based on Nehemiah 8:8—with a sermon proper on a specific text—usually of an hour in duration—later in the service.[10] Obviously circumstances to some extent determine length, but one supposes the earlier writers to be nearer the mark of what is reasonable. Still, one should not minimize the general appreciation of Scripture exposition and sermons by congregations in the period.

Order of Service

While the English Book of Common Prayer had early use in Scotland, it is a fixed liturgy, providing a range of fixed prayers and detailed tables of fixed lessons. It is therefore not easy to compare it with the directory. However, the directory does very much follow

8. See Richard Hooker, *Of the Laws of Ecclesiastical Polity* bk. 5.32.3–4, in *Works*, 7th ed. (Oxford: Clarendon Press, 1888), 146–47.

9. The Lutheran and Reformed guideline in the sixteenth century was an exposition no more than one hour in length, although there were exceptions to this rule. Farel was criticized by Calvin for his long sermons, and Olevianus typically preached for ninety minutes—see Joel R. Beeke's introduction to *The Decades of Henry Bullinger* (Grand Rapids: Reformation Heritage, 2004), 1:xcii. In the 1580s Andrew Melville in Scotland describes the Sunday service, which he approved as fitting within an hour and a half, McMillan, *Worship*, 145. By the 1630s the service was much extended with reading and singing before the preacher entered, so as to run perhaps three hours in all, including a sermon of an hour's duration, ibid., 129.

10. The practice in New England is well described in Hughes Oliphant Old, *The Reading and Preaching of the Scriptures in the Worship of the Christian Church*, vol. 5 (Grand Rapids: Eerdmans, 2004), 170ff.

the Book of Common Order used in Scotland from 1564, which is derived from John Knox's *Forme of Prayers* used in the English Congregation in Geneva. In this book there is discretion in the wording of the prayers and no fixed lectionary.

It is to be noted that the Lord's Supper is not part of the ordinary service, as if it is necessary for it to be the climax of Lord's Day worship.

ORDERS OF WORSHIP

Scottish Book of Common Order 1564	Scottish Alex. Henderson 1641[1]	Westminster Directory for Public Worship 1645
Interpretation of the Scriptures		
	(Bell calls to worship)	Call to Worship by minister
Prayer of Confession	Prayer of Approach	Prayer of Approach
	OT Reading NT Reading	OT Reading NT Reading
Metrical Psalm	Metrical Psalms	Metrical Psalm
Prayer for Assistance	Prayer of Confession/ Intercession	Prayer of Confession/ Intercession
	Metrical Psalm	
	Prayer for Blessing of the Word	
Sermon	Sermon	Sermon
Prayer of Intercession	Prayer of Thanksgiving & for Progress of the Gospel	Prayer of Thanksgiving & for Progress of the Gospel
Lord's Prayer	(Lord's Prayer [*or earlier*])	(Lord's Prayer recommended)
Apostles' Creed	(Apostles' Creed)	
Metrical Psalm	Metrical Psalm	Metrical Psalm (if convenient)
Benediction	Benediction	Benediction

1. Details as described in *The Government and Order of the Church of Scotland* (Edinburgh, 1641), 15–17. The afternoon service was similar, but might include exposition of the catechism and catechetical examination.

As the above table demonstrates, the close similarity between Henderson's description of a typical practice in 1641 and what is set out in the directory is evident. The Lord's Prayer was commonly used in his day, recited in unison with the minister, although he doesn't mention it. The recitation of the Apostles' Creed also was common. Both these features, as well as the doxology at the end of the psalms, became casualties of Independent influence from the late 1630s, which many worthies in the Church of Scotland regretted.

There is also not a great difference when compared to the Book of Common Order. This is more obvious when it is realized that the lack of mention of Scripture readings in the service in the 1564 book does not imply that the Scripture was not read—far from it! Indeed, that book provided for a period of reading and exposition of the Scriptures, including time for questions or comments, before the service proper began with the prayer for assistance in the table on the previous page. In practice, the prayer of confession, the singing of psalms, and readings from the Old and New Testaments were the three elements of the service commonly conducted by a reader, and lasting upward of an hour. After this the minister would take over. Readers had been introduced at the time of the Scottish Reformation of 1560 because of the great lack of qualified ministers. It was a temporary expedient, declared by the Assembly of 1580 not to be an ordinary office; but it continued well into the seventeenth century. It was effectively abandoned with the authorization of the directory, to the disappointment of Robert Baillie.[11]

Content

It will be of interest to list the objections to the directory advanced by Dr. Henry Hammond, later chaplain to Charles I, in his *A View of the New Directory and a Vindication of the Ancient Liturgy of the Church of England* issued at Oxford in August 1645. Hammond notes six basic characteristics purposely avoided in the directory: (1) a prescribed form or liturgy, (2) outward or bodily worship, (3) uniformity in worship, (4) the people having a part through responses in prayers, hymns, and readings, (5) the division of prayers into several collects or portions, and (6) ceremonies such as kneeling in communion, the

11. Thomas Leishman, *The Westminster Directory* (Edinburgh: William Blackwood & Sons, 1901), 92, 190–91.

cross in baptism, and the ring in marriage. In respect of (1), this has been covered already. In respect of (2), doting on ceremonies and outward gestures (e.g., bowing to the east) was indeed avoided. As for (3), it was intended that there be uniformity in the parts of worship,[12] though not the words, while in regard to (4) and (5) the directory is not so opposite as Hammond suggests, although it could have been more positive on singing. In regard to (6), kneeling in communion and the cross in baptism had been matters of long and significant controversy between the parties in the Church of England.[13]

Hammond then notes sixteen items avoided in the directory that are more particularly related to the parts of the service: (1) pronouncing of absolution, (2) the necessity of singing psalms and other hymns of the church, (3) the use of the doxology, (4) the use of the ancient creeds, (5) the frequent use of the Lord's Prayer and prayers for the king, (6) saints' days and the Christian year, (7) the reading of the commandments and associated prayers, (8) the order of the offertory, (9) private baptism, (10) a prescribed catechism [this was covered by a later production of the Assembly], (11) confirmation, (12) solemnities of burial for the sake of the living, (13) thanksgiving after childbirth, (14) communion for the sick, (15) the Commination [God's threatenings] service at the beginning of Lent, and (16) the observation of Lent, Rogation days, and the Ember weeks.

Several of these items (1–5, 7, 10) had use in other Reformed churches, but the major items did not. In response to the view that the directory outlines a dull, unimaginative service, Leland Ryken well says:

> Puritan worship resembles the plays of Shakespeare. Shakespeare was content with the scantiest of stage props and built scenery and imagery into the texts of the plays themselves. In a similar

12. Note, contrary to Hammond, William Dell's complaint against Presbyterian uniformity and his plea for unity, not uniformity, in his *Uniformity Examined: Whether it be found in the Gospel or, In the practice of the Churches of Christ* (London: Henry Overton, 1646). Dell had been secretary to Laud. He was ejected in 1662. For a critique of the directory by a Quaker, see the peculiar work of Francis Howgill, *Mistery Babylon the Mother of Harlots Discovered . . .* (London: Thomas Simmons, 1659).

13. See, for example, John Burges, *The Lawfulness of Kneeling in the Act of Receiving the Lord's Supper, Wherein (by the way) also, somewhat of the Crosse in Baptisme* (London: Robert Milbourne, 1631).

way, the Puritan got rid of the "stage scenery" of the Catholic/ Anglican worship and relied on verbal imagery and symbolism, most of it based on the Bible. . . . Once we grant the validity of the verbal image it becomes clear that the Puritan worship service did not starve the imagination or even the senses of the worshipper.[14]

We now turn to consider each item of the directory.

Of Assembling of the Congregation, and their Behaviour in the Public Worship of God

Important emphases here include attendance on the public means of grace (and not neglecting it for private meetings), preparation of heart beforehand, reverence, avoidance of "adoration or bowing themselves toward one place or another,"[15] then the call to worship[16] and opening prayer by the minister.

The reference to "adoration" is explained by the words that follow it. It was forbidding "prayer accompanied by gestures which seemed to recognize a more real presence of the Divine Being in one part of the building than in another."[17] The prelatic party had bowed to the east and to the altar. In Scotland the minister had also customarily knelt in prayer in the pulpit before the service.[18] This the Puritans opposed, but the directory does not condemn it. The Scots regarded it as a lawful custom, but it was laid aside by them in line with the wish of the Westminster Assembly.[19]

14. Leland Ryken, *Worldly Saints* (Grand Rapids: Zondervan, 1986), 125.

15. MSS; there is no comma after "adoration" as in printed texts.

16. A *votum* (Latin: desire) in the form of a Scripture sentence, commonly Ps. 124:8— "Our help is in the name of the LORD, who made the heavens and the earth"—was general in Reformed churches, and could be followed by a call to worship and a salutation or greeting by the minister in the name of the Lord, commonly, "Grace to you and peace from God our Father and from the Lord Jesus Christ." This level of specification is not explicit in the directory. A prayer of approach including confession followed the call to worship in most Reformed liturgies as also in the directory.

17. Leishman, *Westminster Directory*, 86.

18. Curiously enough, the only modern professedly Presbyterian preacher I have seen do this is the Rev. Ian Paisley at his Ravenhill (Belfast) church in 1975.

19. Act of Assembly of the Church of Scotland, February 7, 1645; text most conveniently in Leishman, *Westminster Directory*, 165–69.

So far as actual behavior in worship is concerned, the directory continues:

> The public worship being begun, the people are wholly to attend upon it, forbearing to read any thing, except what the minister is then reading or citing; and abstaining much more from all private whisperings, conferences, salutations, or doing reverence to any person present, or coming in; as also from all gazing, sleeping, and other indecent behaviour, which may disturb the minister or people, or hinder themselves or others in the service of God.

There is no reference to specific postures in worship. As for prayer, Leishman says:

> It is not an unfair generalisation from the facts to say that kneeling was the prevalent attitude of the sixteenth century, that sitting became that of the seventeenth, and standing of the eighteenth.[20]

It is not quite so clear-cut, however, since the materials from which to make assessment are limited and are sometimes capable of more than one interpretation. William McMillan argues that the usual early posture was kneeling.[21] At the Scottish Reformation of 1560 the congregation stood, or sat on stools, forms, or the (typically) earth floor, men and women separately. Private prayer before the service was standing or kneeling. The men would remove their caps during prayers. Apparently the women were not permitted to have their shawls around their heads as it was regarded as "indecent, and a means to provoke sleep," and for the same reason the women were not permitted to lie down.[22] Such rules might seem surprising to us, but given that church attendance was compulsory, one could expect less than ideal behavior, especially in cold and drafty church buildings.

In the 1640s sitting, standing, and kneeling were found with no great debate. Archbishop Leighton of Dunblane complained about the

20. Ibid., 89.
21. McMillan, *Worship*, 151.
22. Ibid., 154–55.

irreverence of sitting in 1666. Leighton favored kneeling, but others, such as Robert McWard, the Covenanter, favored standing, which was indeed common around 1690. The more conservative maintained this posture in the face of the move to sitting, which became general in Scotland by 1875, and in American Old School Presbyterian circles a little earlier.

The directory continues:

> If any, through necessity, be hindered from being present at the beginning, they ought not, when they come into the congregation, to betake themselves to their private devotions, but reverently to compose themselves to join with the assembly in that ordinance of God which is then in hand.

This provision does not prohibit private devotions before the public service begins, but was intended to forbid occupying oneself with private devotions during the public service.

Of Public Reading of the Holy Scriptures

This section of the directory states that reading belongs to the ministerial office. The Scottish Church had been used to readers for the earlier part of the service. By the 1640s they were mainly men who had the ministry in view. The directory permits such to occasionally read and preach, if allowed by the presbytery. This was a concession compared to the norm of Reformed churches, judged by practice in Europe, but more strict than the Independent view. The Independents were in favor of greater lay participation; indeed, the Scots were fearful that the liberty granted to expound would provide an opportunity for lay preaching.

The directory anticipates that the canonical books will be read in order so that "ordinarily, where the reading in either Testament endeth on one Lord's Day, it is to begin the next." The value of this, particularly given low levels of literacy, is obvious. More frequent (additional) reading of books like the book of Psalms is recommended. Any exposition is to follow the reading, not to be interspersed with it. This statement was not a *direction* to add expository comments, but

121

was soon elaborated in Scotland to an extended lecture/commentary distinct from the subsequent sermon, a practice already common among the Independents in England. In effect the "double sermon" embodied two traditions—the exposition of Scripture favored by the early Reformers and a doctrinal discourse on an isolated text more usual in the pre-Reformation context.[23] Indeed, strange as it may seem, reading of Scripture as a distinct element in worship was widely absent from Scottish services until the nineteenth century, being swallowed up by the expository comments—hence the direction of the Established Church of Scotland Assembly in 1856.[24]

The reading was to be from "the best allowed translation." While the King James Version of 1611 was widely used, the Geneva (1560) still had a following. There was a measure of dissatisfaction with the KJV by some Puritans who desired a more thorough revision.

The Commons added a paragraph at the end of this section exhorting the private reading of the Scriptures, that those who could not read learn to do so, and that all have a Bible.

Prayer

A little over 25 percent of the words in the directory are devoted to suggested content of the prayers, half of this in the prayer before the sermon, although there was the option to include parts of this prayer in that after the sermon. The outlines are richly detailed.

The prayer of approach is to acknowledge God's "incomprehensible greatness and majesty" and our vileness, unworthiness, and utter inability. It seeks pardon, assistance, and acceptance, and a blessing on the Scripture to be read, all in the name and mediation of the Lord Jesus Christ.

The prayer before the sermon moves through the following themes:

1. Acknowledging our great sinfulness.

23. This is the hypothesis of Old, *The Reading and Preaching of the Scriptures*, 5:28–30.
24. In 1856 ministers were enjoined "to observe the recommendations contained in it respecting the reading of the Scriptures of the Old and New Testament at each diet of worship," and the hope is also expressed "that the principles maintained in that Directory will be duly observed."

2. Bewailing our blindness and hardness of heart.

3. Acknowledging we are justly unworthy of the smallest of God's benefits, but fully worthy of God's fiercest wrath.

4. Notwithstanding, drawing near to the throne of grace in the riches and all-sufficiency of the satisfaction and intercession of Christ, confident of the promises of the new covenant, and humbly seeking for mercy and remission of sins only for the sake of the bitter sufferings and precious merits of our only Savior.

5. Praying for the gracious influences of the Holy Spirit, in pardoning and assurance binding up of the broken-hearted; and for the presumptuous, that they might be convicted and brought out of darkness into light.

6. Praying for sanctification, and grace to fit and enable for the duties of life and our calling toward God and man.

7. Praying for the spread of the Gospel, the conversion of the Jews, the fullness of the Gentiles, the fall of Antichrist, and the hastening of the second coming of our Lord; for persecuted and oppressed churches overseas, and for the kingdoms united in the Solemn League and Covenant.

8. Praying for the Sovereign and for other leaders in Church and State at home and overseas.

9. Praying for right use of the sacraments and of God's holy Sabbath.

10. Praying that we be profitable hearers of the Word, growing in grace and knowledge, deepening our communion with the Lord.

11. And that the minister may be given wisdom, faithfulness, zeal and suitable words to minister to the congregations aright, and that the Lord would give the hearers attentive ears, and their hearts established in every good word and work for ever.

The prayer after sermon includes:

1. Thanks for the love of God and the blessings of the gospel.

2. For the spread of the gospel; the chief and most useful heads of the sermon to be turned into a few petitions that they may abide in the heart and bring forth fruit.

3. For preparation for death, judgment, the return of Christ; and for forgiveness for the sins of our holy things, all through the merit and mediation of our great High Priest and Savior.

The Lord's Prayer, "being not only a pattern of prayer but itself a most comprehensive prayer," is recommended for use in the prayers of the church. This was a common position in England[25] and accorded with Scottish practice also. However, the impact of English Independents had been felt in Scotland from the late 1630s, and the Lord's Prayer soon fell into disuse there.[26] The Independents at the Assembly were very much against fixed prayers. Nevertheless, Philip Nye, one of their number, pointed out that there is a middle way between

25. Note, for example, William Gouge, *A Guide to goe to God, or an explanation of the perfect Patterne of Prayer, the Lord's Prayer* (London, 1626, 1636). Gouge (1578–1653) was a leading Puritan and member of the Assembly. In the preface he writes, "It is not only a most absolute prayer in itself, but also a perfect pattern for other prayers"; and on page 4, "the common custom of concluding our own prayers with this perfect form of prayer prescribed by the Lord is very commendable."

26. The use of the Lord's Prayer in the public worship of Presbyterian Scotland by many came to be regarded as an obnoxious prelatic superfluity, although it was agreeable to the directory, and its use, and that of the Apostles' Creed and the Ten Commandments, as resolved by St. Mary's Whitekirk in 1698, can be seen as within the generally admitted jurisdiction of a session. The famous James Hog of Carnock wrote in 1705 of the use of the Lord's Prayer in public worship as "an engine of hell." The Assembly of 1705 passed an act recommending close following of the directory at the instance of Sir Hugh Calder, who strongly advocated the use of the Lord's Prayer, yet it declined to specifically recommend its use. The anecdote concerning Rev. Patrick Simson of Renfrew, the former Covenanter who had suffered under episcopacy, is noteworthy. As part of a communion service in 1710 he took the opportunity to observe that there were three things that had Christ's name particularly given them: The Lord's Day, the Lord's Supper, and the Lord's Prayer. After he had spoken a while on the former two, he spoke a little upon the use of the Lord's Prayer, and first repeated it, and then prayed over the different petitions, enlarging on each at some length. His explanation was that for several days before the communion he had had a strong impression on his spirit that he should testify his communion with the whole Christian church by the public use of the Lord's Prayer. Further, he was now 82 years old, and many of the young ministers might claim that they never heard the old men use the Lord's Prayer and so make this a further excuse for its total disuse, which he thought a fault, though he was against the abuse of it. See W. D. Maxwell, *A History of Worship in the Church of Scotland* (Oxford: Oxford University Press, 1955), 130–39.

set forms and extemporaneous prayers: "I plead for neither, but for studied prayers."[27]

The benediction is not a prayer, but a blessing; thus the common Scottish practice of ministers, using "be with you" rather than "be with us" (other than in the General Assembly).[28] Nevertheless, other Reformed churches have commonly used "be with us" in the ordinary service.

Singing of Psalms

The singing of psalms perhaps does not receive quite the prominence one might have expected. On the surface it is not thought essential, and the Scottish First *Book of Discipline* (1560) had so described it.[29] The directory refers to the first psalm thus: "After reading of the word (and singing of the psalm)," and the second after the prayer following the sermon thus: "The prayer ended, let a psalm be sung, if with conveniency it may be done." So one psalm only is seen as the norm in the ordinary course with an additional optional one—perhaps this should be taken as a minimum. On the other hand, singing of psalms is considered appropriate for the Lord's Day outside the times of public worship, and for days of fasting and thanksgiving.

Preaching of the Word

Some 12 percent of the directory is taken up by a fine section on preaching. We might be surprised to find a section on preaching in a

27. Murray in *To Glorify & Enjoy God*, 187, citing Mitchell, *Westminster Assembly*, 229. Note Philip Henry's agreement with the directory, *The Lives of Philip and Matthew Henry* (Edinburgh: Banner of Truth, 1974), 142.

28. Cf. Leishman, *Westminster Directory*, 104.

29. Chapter 11.1 states that singing of psalms is not essential to the "face of the visible kirk." Though "profitable," it is not "necessary," for "in some kirks the psalms may conveniently be sung, in others perchance they cannot . . ." Note Henry Hammond's comment that singing of psalms in meter is not prescribed "making it very indifferent, it seems, whether it be kept at all in the Church or no . . ." *A View of the New Directory*, 31. But compare the Westminster Confession 21.5 composed two years later. The first Scottish Psalter (1564) had a lot of awkward versification, 27 meters, and 105 tunes, and was beyond the capacity of most congregations. Most editions after 1622 did not include the music. In the metropolitan area psalm-singing had ceased by the 1640s (cf. Millar Patrick, *Four Centuries of Scottish Psalmody* [London: Oxford University Press, 1950], 81).

directory for public worship, and in the Westminster Assembly some held it to be needless. On the other hand, Van Dixhoorn rightly states: "Yet the Assembly, in a rare display of initiative, determined that preaching was important enough and bad preaching common enough that some directives were necessary."[30] The spread of sectaries in the 1640s who downplayed preaching, or else rejected the necessity of a well-trained ministry, is relevant. Drawing largely on the influential work of the Puritan William Perkins (1558–1602), the three-part structure of exegesis, raising of doctrines, and application of them is advanced. The directory stresses the spiritual qualifications of the minister, the importance of cultivating his gifts, and the importance of private preparation.

The method of preaching outlined had been found by experience to be much blessed by God and helpful to the people, but it is not prescribed as necessary for everyone. The preaching may be based on a single text or a more extended passage and be part of a consecutive series or an occasional text.[31] The introduction is to be brief, the text should be briefly summarized, and the analysis is to be clear and simple. The doctrines derived are to be true doctrines, and the doctrines in the text; and the preacher is to concentrate on the principal doctrines in the text and state them plainly, using pertinent parallel places of Scriptures as appropriate. He is to use solid, convincing arguments, and any illustrations should "convey the truth into the hearer's heart with spiritual delight." Difficulties should be handled, but only those that are relevant in the circumstances. Doctrine should not be stated so generally that it is not applied to the hearers, a difficult task requiring prudence, zeal, and meditation.

The uses drawn from the doctrines may be confirmed when suitable by a few further arguments from the text or other Scriptures. In refuting error "he is neither to raise an old heresy from the grave, nor to mention a blasphemous opinion unnecessarily." In teaching duties he is to show also the means to perform them. He is to show,

30. Chad Van Dixhoorn, *A Puritan Theology of Preaching* (London: St. Antholin's Lectureship, 2005), 14.
31. The evidence favors the view that preaching from a doctrinal proposition or from a catechism was rejected by the Westminster divines. A biblical text was required as the foundation of the sermon.

when there is reason, the nature and greatness of sin, but also the danger his hearers are in, together with the remedies and the best way to avoid it. In bringing comfort he is "carefully to answer such objections as a troubled heart and afflicted spirit may suggest to the contrary." He is to seek, circumspectly and prudently, keeping close to Scripture, to aid his hearers in self-examination so that they might be humbled for their sins and strengthened with comfort as their situation may require. He need not expound every doctrine in his text, but is to make wise choices as to what is needful and appropriate so as to draw their souls to Christ. One may justly say that the preacher in this view is considered to be a soul-physician.

Whatever method is used, the minister is to carry out his whole ministry painstakingly, not negligently, plainly, so that the uneducated can follow him, in demonstration of the Spirit, using citations from other languages or writers sparingly. He is to be faithful, seeking Christ's honor, not his own, and the salvation and edification of the people. He is to be wise, using means most likely to be effective, with due respect for each one, and the avoidance of his own passions and bitterness. He is to be a person of gravity, exercising his ministry with loving concern and godly zeal to do his hearers good. He is to be an embodiment of what he preaches, both in public and in private.

Baptism

The section on baptism assumes a Christian nation and envisages infant baptism as the norm. The child is to be presented for baptism in the public worship service soon after birth by the father, or by a Christian friend if the father is unavoidably absent. The meaning of the sacrament is to be explained, the congregation and the parent suitably exhorted, prayer offered (in which request is made that the Lord "would join the inward baptism of his Spirit with the outward baptism of water"), the child baptized with water, and so received "into the bosom of the visible church," with a prayer of blessing in conclusion.

The common practice in Scotland was for baptism to be administered on the second Lord's Day after the birth, and with rare and controverted exceptions,[32] the baptism was always in the presence of the congregation. In England, the large majority of baptisms were private, and it was common for the midwife to present the child for baptism;[33] so there was a definite acceptance of the Scots' position at these points. Fonts in older pre-Reformation churches were at the doors; this was discountenanced as unsuited for baptism in the face of the congregation. It was common for the parent to hold up the child to be baptized by the minister from the pulpit, and in Scotland the sacrament was administered at the close of the sermon.

The directory requires the parent's "solemn promise for the performance of his duty."

In the original submission to Parliament this read:

"It is recommended to the parent or the Christian friend to make a profession of his faith by answering to these or like questions. Dost thou believe in God the Father, Son and Holy Ghost? Dost thou hold thyself bound to observe all that Christ hath commanded thee, and wilt thou endeavour to so do? Dost thou desire to have this child baptised into the faith and profession of Jesus Christ?"

These questions had been agreed in October.[34] However, at the General Assembly of the Church of Scotland in February 1645 it was proposed they be dropped, and the adjustment was duly made before final printing. The questions were virtually implied in the preceding text, but it may well be that the Scots thought not to disturb the varieties of practice among themselves, particularly the recitation by the parent of the Apostles' Creed, a custom not used in England. At root the issue over the questions may be seen to be about the kind of profession required. Was it a profession of regeneration on the part of the parent or something less? The final wording seems intended to prevent scruples by adherents of different viewpoints. Both the directory and the confession have been regarded as implying a profession of saving faith by the

32. For examples see McMillan, *Worship*, 254ff.
33. Leishman, *Westminster Directory*, 106, citing Robert Baillie.
34. George Gillespie, *Notes of Proceedings of the Assembly of Divines at Westminster* (Edinburgh: Robert Ogle, Oliver & Boyd, 1846), 91.

parent as giving the right to baptism for the child.[35] In practice baptism could be and was administered on the basis of profession of a parent in an earlier generation, a practice that Samuel Rutherford defended at length, but that others, such as Thomas Boston, opposed. The ideal of a Christian nation and the existence of a single Christian church obviously impacted early thought.

It is important to note that the child is regarded as having a right to the covenant sign because of the covenant promise: "That the promise is made to believers and their seed; and that the seed and posterity of the faithful, born within the Church, have, by their birth, interest in the covenant." Again, "they are Christians, and federally holy before baptism, and therefore are they baptised." They are members of the church, subject to its oversight. The expectation should be that they grow up to profess their faith, and, as now able to examine themselves, to participate in the Lord's Supper. The emphasis on thorough Christian training rather than sporadic special efforts is evident.[36]

As regards mode, the Assembly specified in the directory that the minister

> is to baptize the child with water, which for the manner of doing is not only lawful but expedient to be by pouring or sprinkling water on the face of the child, without any other ceremony.

In debate the previous day (August 7, 1644) the proposal to include dipping as well as pouring and sprinkling was excluded

35. Note William Cunningham's assessment: "no infants ought to be baptized, except those of persons who ought themselves to be baptized as adults upon their own profession, and who, being thus recognised as believers, are not only entitled, but bound, to be habitually receiving the Lord's Supper," *The Reformers and the Theology of the Reformation* (Edinburgh, 1862), 290. This is Boston's view in part arising from a protest against formalism and false peace. On the other hand the earlier Scottish writers, motivated by care to avoid applying to the visible church what belonged to the invisible, and by concern for the salvation of sinners, argued that a profession of faith was sufficient if it was a serious willingness to sit under the preaching of the gospel and the care of the church officers. See Samuel Rutherford, *A Peaceable and Temperate Plea for Paul's Presbyterie in Scotland* (London: John Bartlet, 1642), 164ff.; cf. John Macpherson, *The Doctrine of the Church in Scottish Theology* (Edinburgh: Macniven & Wallace, 1903), 80–90.

36. Despite some weaknesses in the historical reconstruction, a valuable study of the significance of baptism is L. B. Schenck, *The Presbyterian Doctrine of Children in the Covenant* (1940, repr. Phillipsburg, NJ: P&R Publishing, 2003). See my review in *The Confessional Presbyterian* 2 (2006): 181–84.

twenty-five votes to twenty-four. It should be noted that the debate was not between dipping and the other modes, as is sometimes stated, but on the propriety of putting dipping on the same level as the other modes. The next day the question was dealt with afresh and the statement above agreed to. "But as for the dispute itself about dipping, it was thought fit and most safe to let it alone."[37] The Westminster Confession takes a similar line and teaches that "dipping of the person into the water is not necessary" [28.3]. Pouring or sprinkling is sufficient. It is difficult to suppose that placing immersion on the same level as affusion would have made any more difference in practice than has the rubric in the English Prayer Book: "he shall dip it in the Water discreetly and warily"—which is observed in the breach.

Lord's Supper

The directory requires the "frequent" observance of the Lord's Supper, generally after the morning sermon, but how often is to be decided by the local session as they consider appropriate for the comfort and edification of the people.[38] Knox's Liturgy of 1556, reflecting the practice of the congregation of English exiles in Geneva, includes a rubric, "The Lord's Supper is commonly administered once a month, or so oft as the congregation shall think expedient." However, the First Book of Discipline of 1560, while recognizing the sufficiency of the order of Geneva (2.2), added more specific instruction: "Four times a year we think sufficient for the administration of the Lord's table, which we desire to be distincted [distinguished/specified], that the superstitions of times may be avoided as far as may be . . ." (11.5).

37. John Lightfoot, *Journal of the Westminster Assembly* in *Works* (1834 ed.), 13:301; cf. my *Baptism in Scripture & History* (Melbourne: 1992), 55–56.

38. George Gillespie records: "But the Committee went through in order; and first, objection was made against that first section, which leaves to the discretion of the pastor and elders of each congregation how oft the communion is to be celebrated. It was desired that they might be tied, at least, to four times a-year, since the Apostle and Christ speak of often celebration. I said, There is no ground from Scripture or otherwise to determine four times a year, for this should resolve in the arbitrement of men. If congregations abuse this liberty, the presbytery at visitation of churches can help it. Mr Newcomen declared that all the new gathered churches have the sacrament every Lord's day in the afternoon. To avoid this debate of the time, it was added in the beginning, *The Lord's Supper is to be administered frequently.*" *Notes of Proceedings of the Assembly*, 102.

Anxious to avoid the observance of the Supper at Easter, which many thought gave special virtue to it, the Book of Discipline specified the first Sunday in each of March, June, September, and December. It added, "We do not deny but any several kirk for reasonable causes may change the time, and may minister more often, but we study [earnestly endeavour] to repress superstition." In 1562 the General Assembly ordained that the communion be celebrated four times in the year within towns, and twice in the year in the country.[39] Even so, with the shortage of ministers, frequency was often far less, even once a year, sometimes spread over several Sundays if the population was large. The usage of the Independents of the 1640s of a weekly communion was one that did not impact in Scotland, and frequency in Scotland was commonly annual for a considerable period.

Practice in the Church of England could accommodate a greater frequency. The Prayer Book (1559) and Canons (1603) were for at least three times a year, but in practice few communicated more than once, and then at Easter. William Pemble (1591–1623) wrote:

Satan hath done much by his malicious policy to corrupt men's hearts in the observance of it: when the Sacrament was administered often he brought it into contempt by the commonness of it; now that it is administered seldom through ignorance, it is abused and neglected as unnecessary.[40]

Pemble lamented that if there had been no civil law requiring attendance at least once a year, the Lord's Table would be left without guests. Communion practice declined with the ejection of nonconformists to the new order of 1662, as they were often the more committed people, and monthly communion was found among them.

The directory specified that "the ignorant and the scandalous are not fit to receive" the Lord's Supper. The original wording was ordered omitted by Parliament. It read:

39. David Calderwood, *History of the Kirk of Scotland*, vol. 2 (Edinburgh:Wodrow Society, 1843), 209.

40. William Pemble, *An Introduction to the Worthy Receiving the sacrament of the Lord's Supper* (London, 1629), 5. There is a valuable article by Arnold Hunt entitled "The Lord's Supper in Early Modern England" in *Past & Present* for November 1998, accessible at http://www.findarticles.com/p/articles/mi_m2279/is_1998_Nov/ai_53542829.

> None are to be admitted thereunto but such as being baptised are found upon careful examination by the minister, before the other church officers, to have a competent measure of knowledge and ability to examine themselves, and do propose their willingness to submit themselves to all the ordinances of Christ. The ignorant, the scandalous, the obstinate are not to be admitted; nor those of another congregation except they have sufficient testimony or be very well known.

In Scotland the omitted words were largely offset by the Supplementary Act to the act approving the directory. Passed by the Church of Scotland Assembly on February 7, 1645, this act requires trial and examination of congregations before the communion, according to the past practice.[41]

The directory envisages a preparation address on the Lord's Day previous to or during the week before the communion. The Scottish Supplementary Act specified that this be the day before. After his sermon and prayer the directory requires a short "exhortation, warning and invitation" (commonly called the "fencing" of the table[42]) prior to the celebration of the Supper. After it "the minister may, in a few words, put them in mind of the grace of God in Jesus Christ held forth in this sacrament, and exhort them to work worthy of it." The Supplementary Act states that there was to be only one address before communicating and one thanksgiving address regardless of the number of sittings, but there could be "a short exhortation" or "some few short sentences" at each sitting. Singing of psalms was to occur while people were coming to or leaving the table.[43] The elaboration of table addresses and pre- and post-communion services beyond this, still found in some places, is a later development.

The point that caused the most debate of anything in the directory was the manner of receiving communion. The Scots sat around a long

41. Text in Leishman, *Westminster Directory*, 165–69.
42. In Scots Presbyterianism the descriptive phrase "he fences and opens the tables" is used by Steuart of Pardovan, in his collection of church law and practice published in 1709, to describe the commencement of the Lord's Supper service by the minister. "Fencing the table" in the early sense is not simply a negative prohibition to deter unworthy communicants but involves a positive stating of the warrant to partake.
43. Text in Leishman, *Westminster Directory*, 165–69.

table in the front of the church, with successive sittings if there were more communicants than could be seated at one time. The English generally sat in the pews, and the elements of bread and wine were brought to them. The Scots were insistent on the importance of their practice as illustrating being at a feast with Christ. After more than two weeks' debate, in which neither side gave ground, the final wording "about it, or at it" was intended to cover both practices.[44] This is an example of how those agreed on the regulative principle could disagree on its application. Other interesting points in the directory include the sanctifying and blessing of the elements by the Word and prayer, and the prayer of thanksgiving. There is also the breaking of the bread after the consecration prayer, and the provision of "large cups" for the wine.[45] The theology of the Supper is set out in the Confession of Faith.

At this point the divines signed the document, added the preface, signed the next section on the Lord's Day separately, and submitted these items to Parliament, November 20, 1644. They then proceeded to draft the remaining sections.

Of the Sanctification of the Lord's Day

This section is straightforward. The whole day is identified as the Christian Sabbath. All are to abstain from all unnecessary labors, yet the implication is that servants will have necessary labors that are to be so arranged so as to not unnecessarily detain them from attendance at public worship. On the whole the section is quite positively written. The question of church discipline on the Lord's Day, which was usual in Scotland, was raised but not determined in the directory.

The Solemnization of Marriage

Marriage is to involve mutual consent on the part of those of years of discretion, and parental consent is in all cases desirable and not to

---

44. The Assembly manuscript includes after "at it" "(as in the Church of Scotland)," but this disappears in the final text. The Scottish practice of sitting at the table was changed in the nineteenth century largely through the influence of Dr. Thomas Chalmers, who provided special pews in the new St. John's Church, Glasgow (1819), to facilitate communicating in the pew.

45. The "common cup" was not so common that there was invariably only one cup.

be unreasonably withheld. While Independents thought of marriage as a civil contract with the minister acting for the civil authority, the first paragraph of the directory rises higher than this while rejecting the idea of marriage as a sacrament. The words "in the place appointed by Authority for public worship" originally read "in the place of the public meeting of the congregation," but the change was made at the request of the Scottish Church so as to exclude places of worship not recognized by the then ruling powers.[46]

Marriage had commonly occurred on the Lord's Day during the service, but the extra work involved contributed to decline of this practice and the recommendation against it in the directory. On the other hand, weddings could be at any time of the year—a phrase probably directed against the old prohibition of marriage during Advent or Lent. After prayer, and a message from Scripture, the vows are said by the parties and they are pronounced man and wife "without any further ceremony"—which is a reference to the use of a ring; the Scots opposed the use of rings because of its pagan origin and use by Rome. A prayer closes the service.

Concerning Visitation of the Sick

This is a quite lengthy pastorally helpful section. Some rewriting occurred between the manuscript as it left the Assembly and the final document, but the effect is largely cosmetic involving some abbreviation and rephrasing. An omission here or in the section on prayer is of any very explicit mention of public prayer for the sick.

Concerning Burial of the Dead

This section was debated over six days. Historically the Reformed Church in Scotland had interred the body of the deceased without any ceremony, the corpse being brought to the place of burial in silence by the relatives and the congregation. In the Scottish Book of Common Order the minister, if present, "maketh some comfortable exhorta-

---

46. Cf. Leishman, *Westminster Directory*, 136. Leishman, following A. F. Mitchell, says "in some church or chapel" was also in the original, but this is not supported by the House of Lords' MSS.

tion to the people touching death and resurrection" in the church, if nearby. Funeral sermons as such were generally discountenanced as likely to "have respect of persons, preaching at the burials of the rich and honourable, but keeping silence when the poor and despised departeth."[47] In England Puritans like Cartwright spoke similarly. However, by the time of the Westminster Assembly funeral services had been forbidden by Act of the Church of Scotland (1638), but were not uncommon in England. All the members of the Assembly at Westminster, except the Scots, attended the funeral of parliamentarian John Pym following his death in 1643. The final form of the directory was held by John Lightfoot to permit funeral sermons,[48] but they remained discountenanced in Scotland and were infrequent for the next 150 years.

Concerning Public Solemn Fasting

In Scotland there had been a practice of fasting at communion times or even the Sunday before communion, but this kind of fasting is passed over, and the fast applies to extraordinary occasions, with special readings and sermons, as well as singing of suitable psalms. It could be noted that the *Form of Church Government* enjoins fasting by the congregation on the day their minister is ordained.

Concerning the Observation of Days of Public Thanksgiving

No comment seems necessary on this section. It provides a good balance, with worship and praise emphasized, as well as enjoyment of refreshments and remembrance of others via the collection referred to.

Of Singing of Psalms

This section describes the singing of psalms as a "duty" in public worship and privately in the family, contra those who scrupled it as

47. *First Book of Discipline*, (1560) 9(4).
48. Leishmann, *Westminster Directory*, 142.

being a paraphrase of Scripture or for other reasons. The voice is to be "tunably and gravely ordered" with the chief care being to sing with understanding and with grace in the heart. It is noted that many cannot read, and so it is appropriate "for the present" for someone to read the psalm line by line before it is sung. Alternate reading and singing, "lining out the psalm," as it was called, was disliked by the Scots and opposed by Alexander Henderson, but it became well established for long after the reason for it had passed. Indeed, it was still found in the early part of the nineteenth century, and is retained in traditional Gaelic psalmody in the Highlands today.

It is very commonly assumed that the statement in the confession, "singing of psalms with grace in the heart," and the references to "psalms" in the directory imply an exclusive psalmody position. This is so only with major qualifications. It was certainly the intention of the Assembly to produce a Psalter as part of the covenanted uniformity, but one should not draw the conclusion that they held the view that only the 150 Psalms of Scripture could properly be used according to the regulative principle. It is abundantly plain that the exegetical tradition was diverse, as was practice, there being about twenty non-Psalter pieces in the *Sternhold & Hopkins* Psalter of 1562 used in the Church of England.[49] There was in Scotland a practical limitation to the Psalter, but an openness to at least other canonical songs, as witnessed by the action of the Assembly of the Church of Scotland in August 1647. The day after approving the new confession, that Assembly took steps to have other Scripture songs translated with a view to public use, something that the troubles of the time delayed, but that was eventually carried through in a modified form in the Scottish Paraphrases of 1781.

A further point is that there was division over the translation of the psalms in meter. The Commons supported the version of Francis Rous, while the Lords supported William Barton's version (as did

49. For discussion see my *Psalms in Christian Worship* (Melbourne: Presbyterian Church of Eastern Australia, 1992); also Rowland S. Ward, "Psalms and Hymns?" in *The Monthly Record of the Free Church of Scotland*, January 2002, 4–6. Dr. Nick Needham convincingly demonstrates the case at length in "Westminster and Worship: Psalms, Hymns? and Musical Instruments?" in *The Westminster Confession into the 21st Century*, ed. J. Ligon Duncan, vol 2. (Fearn: Mentor, 2004), 223–306.

the London ministers). Ultimately, Rous' version was revised by the Assembly with input from Scotland, approved by the Commons, and printed in April 1646. The House of Commons ordered its exclusive use in England and Wales from January 1 following. But it did not supplant Sternhold and Hopkins,[50] nor was the Scottish Church satisfied. The Westminster version was further revised in Scotland over the space of two years and four months to produce what we know as the Scottish Psalter of 1650. However, only 10 percent of the lines are from Rous and a little under 20 percent from the Westminster version. It is in fact a mosaic drawn from about a dozen other versions, with about 40 percent from the Scottish revisers.[51] It is therefore quite misleading in modern discussions to term the Scottish Psalter Rous' Psalter or an English production, although it was often called Rous' "Metaphrase" at the time.

AN APPENDIX: Touching Days and Places of Public Worship

Having some spare time one November day, the divines decided to deal with this subject, and the following month the section was agreed to. Festival days, commonly called holy days, were to be discontinued as lacking foundation in the Word of God. The Reformation had brought about a major change in the observance of holy days. Days dedicated to saints were universally abandoned, but the great festivals—Christmas, Easter Day, Ascension Day, and Pentecost—were retained, but stripped of superstitious accretions. However, this was not the case in Scotland, where "because in God's Scriptures they neither have commandment nor assurance, we judge them utterly abolished from this Realm."[52] In 1566 the General Assembly heartily approved the Helvetic Confession except that part (art. 24) concerning "the festivals of our Lord's nativity, circumcision, passion, resurrection, ascension and sending the Holy Spirit upon his disciples,"

---

50. The suggestion that it was too Scottish has been made—Millar Patrick, *Four Centuries*, 96.
51. Note the details drawn from W. P. Rorison's analysis in Millar Patrick, *Four Centuries*, 102.
52. First Book of Discipline (1560), 1.

stating, "we dare not religiously celebrate any other feast day than what the Divine articles have prescribed."[53] The National Covenant of 1581 also condemned "dedicating of kirks, altars, days, vows to creatures," but in 1618 King James forced on the church the Five Articles of Perth,[54] one of which enjoined the devout observance of certain holy days. So we have both the superstitions of Rome and the imposition of a king involved in the feelings on this subject. Some, including Robert Baillie, did not regard such days to be condemned by the National Covenant as positively unlawful. While Henderson disagreed with this, he refused to condemn other Reformed churches that observed them.[55]

Conclusion

The directory obviously contains some dated material, and yet, even where it may not be followed today with the care originally intended, it offers wise counsel. We may not have the same concern to avoid funeral services, yet who can deny that there are dangers in our own time with them? We do not think of a ring in marriage as a hangover from popery, nor become passionate over whether we sit in the pew or around a table at the Lord's Supper, but it was high views of marriage and of the Supper that led to strongly held opinions on these matters. We should have high views too, even if the application is seen in a different light today. In an age when the written word is losing out to the visual, reading two chapters in course has a lot of logic, particularly where people are not literate or not biblically literate. Hopefully, we don't have the same negative reaction to the use of the Lord's Prayer as some did, and heed the advice in the directory. We might be well advantaged to dispatch any announcements before the services lest they intrude in a way the directory does not recognize, and to also keep in view the problems of lengthy communion services that have developed

53. Cited from McMillan, *Worship*, 301.
54. The articles provided for (1) kneeling during communion, (2) private baptism, (3) private communion for the sick or infirm, (4) confirmation by a bishop, and (5) the devout observance of five holy days: Christ's birth, death, resurrection, ascension, and Pentecost.
55. McMillan, *Worship*, 327.

in some circles since the 1640s. We may find Christmas and Easter to be days of opportunity in a multicultural and secular context in Western societies of today, even if we agree that they are not required by Scripture. Those of Scots background may be challenged as to whether New Year services cannot sometimes be associated with a kind of worldliness and superstition the Westminster divines would have roundly condemned.

The directory is a much-neglected but extremely valuable part of the work of the Westminster divines. One can hardly do better than quote the greatest of the professors of Old Princeton Seminary, B. B. Warfield. He writes:

At this distance of time we may look upon it dispassionately; and, so viewed, it can scarcely fail to commend itself as an admirable set of agenda, in spirit and matter alike well fitted to direct the public services of a great Church. It is notable for its freedom from petty prescriptions and "superfluities" and for the emphasis it places upon what is specifically commanded in the Scriptures. Its general tone is lofty and spiritual; its conception of acceptable worship is sober and restrained and at the same time profound and rich; the paradigms of prayer which it offers are notably full and yet free from over-elaboration, compressed and yet enriched by many reminiscences of the best models which had preceded them; and it is singular among agenda for the dominant place it gives in the public worship of the Church to the offices of reading and preaching the Word. To both of these offices it vindicates a place, and a prominent place, among the parts of public worship, specifically so called, claiming for them distinctively a function in inducing and expressing that sense of dependence of God and of subjection to Him in which all religion is rooted and which is the purest expression of worship; and thus justifying in the ordering of the public services of the churches the recognition of the Word as a means, perhaps we should say the means, of grace. It expends as much care upon the minister's proper performance of the offices of reading and preaching the Word, therefore, as upon his successful performance of the duty of leading the congregation in prayer and acceptably administering to it the Sacraments. The paragraph of the Preaching of the Word is in effect, indeed, a complete homiletical treatise, remarkable at once for its sober

139

practical sense and its profound spiritual wisdom and suffused with a tone of sincere piety, and of zeal at once for the truth and for the souls which are to be bought with the truth.[56]

One can only say, "Amen."

56. B. B. Warfield, *The Westminster Assembly and its Work* (New York: Oxford University Press, 1932), 51–52.

Appendix:
A Directory for the Public Worship of God in the Three Kingdoms[1]

Table of Contents

1. The text is reproduced with modern spelling and an approximation of modern punctuation from the MSS and the amendments of Parliament, with more modern equivalents for certain words indicated in brackets following them. The relatively few examples of –eth endings have been eliminated, "Spirit" substituted for "Ghost" in two instances, and "conveniency" rendered as "convenience." In the Preface only, long sentences have on several occasions been broken up to improve readability. The document could be rewritten in modern English style, but I have tried to balance the desirability of such a text with the competing claims of an original text. It does not appear that there are significant deficiencies in most printed editions, although, as far as I know, the variations from the original MSS given in the footnotes have not been noted before in such editions.

The Preface

In the beginning of the blessed Reformation, our wise and pious ancestors took care to set forth an order for redress of many things which they then, by the Word, discovered to be vain, erroneous, superstitious, and idolatrous in the public worship of God. This occasioned many godly and learned men to rejoice much in the *Book of Common Prayer*, at that time set forth because the Mass and the rest of the Latin service being removed, the public worship was celebrated in our own tongue. Many of the common people also received benefit by hearing the Scriptures read in their own language, which formerly were unto them as a book that is sealed.

Nevertheless, long and sad experience has made it manifest [plain] that the Liturgy used in the Church of England, notwithstanding all the pains and religious intentions of the compilers of it, has proved an offence not only to many of the godly at home, but also to the Reformed Churches abroad. For, not to speak of insistence on the reading of all the prayers, which very greatly increased the burden of it, the many unprofitable and burdensome ceremonies contained in it have occasioned much mischief, both by disquieting [making uneasy] the consciences of many godly ministers and people, who could not yield [submit] unto them, and by depriving them of the ordinances of God, which they might not enjoy without conforming or subscribing to those ceremonies. By these means numbers of good Christians have been kept from the Lord's table, and various able and faithful ministers debarred from the exercise of their ministry, to the endangering of many thousand souls in a time of such scarcity of faithful pastors, and spoiled of their livelihood, to the undoing of them and their families. Prelates, and their faction, have labored to raise the estimation of it to such a height as if there were no other worship, or way of worship, of God among us but only the Service-book. This has been to the great hindrance of the preaching of the Word, and in some places, especially of late, to the jostling of it out as unnecessary or (at best) as far inferior to the reading of Common Prayer. This was made no better than an idol by many ignorant and superstitious people who, pleasing [congratulating] themselves in their presence at that service, and their lip-labor in bearing a part in it, have

142

in this way hardened themselves in their ignorance and carelessness of saving knowledge and true piety.

In the meantime, Papists boasted that the book was a compliance with them [complying with their desire] in a great part of their service, and so were not a little confirmed in their superstition and idolatry, expecting rather our return to them than endeavoring the reformation of themselves. In this expectation they were of late very much encouraged when, upon the pretended warrantableness [claimed authority] of imposing the former ceremonies, new ones were daily obtruded [pushed] upon the Church.

Add to this, which was not foreseen but has since come to pass, that the Liturgy has been a great means as on the one hand to make and increase an idle and unedifying ministry; it contented itself with set forms made to their hands by others without putting forth themselves to exercise the gift of prayer, with which our Lord Jesus Christ is pleased to furnish all His servants whom He calls to that office. On the other side, the Liturgy has been, and ever would be, if continued, a matter of endless strife and contention in the Church, and a snare both to many godly and faithful ministers who have been persecuted and silenced upon that occasion [because of this], and to others of hopeful parts [likely gifts]. Many of them have been diverted, and more still would be, from all thoughts of the ministry to other studies. Especially is this so in these latter times in which God vouchsafes [condescends to grant] to His people more and better means for the discovery of error and superstition, and for attaining of knowledge in the mysteries of godliness, and gifts in preaching and prayer.

[It is] upon these and many the like weighty considerations in reference to the whole book in general, and because of divers [various] particulars contained in it, [and] not any love to novelty, or intention to disparage our first Reformers, of whom we are persuaded that, were they now alive, they would join with us in this work. We acknowledge them as excellent instruments raised by God to begin the purging and building of his House, and desire they may be had of us and posterity in everlasting remembrance, with thankfulness and honor. But that we may in some measure answer the gracious providence of God, which at this time calls upon us for further reformation, and may satisfy our own consciences, and answer the expectation of other Reformed

Churches, and the desires of many of the godly among ourselves, and withal [as well] give some public testimony of our endeavors for uniformity in divine worship which we have promised in our Solemn League and Covenant, we have, after earnest and frequent calling on the name of God, and after much consultation, not with flesh and blood, but with his holy Word, resolved to lay aside the former Liturgy, with the many rites and ceremonies formerly used in the worship of God, and have agreed on this following Directory for all the parts of public worship, at ordinary and extraordinary times.

In it our care has been to hold forth such things as are of divine institution in every ordinance; and other things we have endeavoured to set forth according to the rules of Christian prudence, agreeable to the general rules of the Word of God. Our intention being only that the general heads, the sense and scope of the prayers, and other parts of public worship being known to all, there may be a consent of all the churches in those things that contain the substance of the service and worship of God. Also that the ministers may be directed by it in their administrations, to keep like soundness in doctrine and prayer, and may, if need be, have some help and illustration, but in such a way that they do not become slothful and negligent in stirring up the gifts of Christ in them. Rather, our aim is that each one, by meditation, by taking heed to himself and the flock of God committed to him, and by wise observing the ways of Divine Providence, may be careful to furnish his heart and tongue with further or other materials of prayer and exhortation, as shall be needed on all occasions.

A Directory for Public Prayer, Reading the Holy Scriptures, Singing of Psalms, Preaching of the Word, Administration of the Sacraments, and Other Parts of the Public Worship of God, Ordinary and Extraordinary

Of the Assembling of the Congregation, and their Behaviour in the Public Worship of God

WHEN the congregation is to meet for public worship, the people, having prepared their hearts for it beforehand, ought all to come and join in it, not absenting themselves from the public ordinance through negligence, or on the excuse of private meetings.

Let all enter the assembly, not irreverently, but in a grave and seemly manner, taking their seats or places without adoration, or bowing themselves towards one place or other.

The congregation being assembled, the minister, after solemn calling on them to the worshipping of the great name of God, is to begin with prayer.

In all reverence and humility, acknowledging the incomprehensible greatness and majesty of the Lord, in whose presence they do then in a special manner appear, and their own vileness and unworthiness to approach so near him, with their utter inability of themselves to so great a work; and humbly beseeching him for pardon, assistance, and acceptance, in the whole service then to be performed; and for a blessing on that particular portion of his Word then to be read, and all in the name and mediation of the Lord Jesus Christ.

The public worship being begun, the people are wholly to attend on it, forbearing to read any thing, except what the minister is then reading or citing; and abstaining much more from all private whisperings, conferences, greetings, or doing reverence to any person present or coming in; as also from all gazing, sleeping and other indecent behaviour, which may disturb the minister or people or hinder themselves or others in the service of God.

If any, through necessity, be hindered from being present at the beginning, they ought not, when they come into the congregation, engage in their private devotions, but reverently compose themselves to join with the assembly in that ordinance of God which is then in hand.

Of Public Reading of the Holy Scriptures

READING of the Word in the congregation, being part of the public worship of God, in which we acknowledge our dependence on him, and subjection to him, and one means sanctified by him for the edifying of his people, is to be performed by the pastors and teachers. Nevertheless, such as intend the ministry may occasionally both read the Word and exercise their gift in preaching in the congregation, if allowed by the presbytery.

All the canonical books of the Old and New Testament (but none of those which are commonly called Apocrypha) shall be publicly read in the common language, out of the best allowed translation, distinctly, that all may hear and understand.

How large a portion shall be read at once is left to the wisdom of the minister. It is appropriate that ordinarily one chapter of each Testament is read at every meeting, and sometimes more, where the chapters are short or the coherence of matter [the content] requires it.

It is necessary that all the canonical books be read over in order, so that the people may be better acquainted with the whole body of the scriptures. Normally, where the reading in either Testament ends on one Lord's Day, it is to begin the next. We commend also the more frequent reading of such scriptures as he that reads shall think best for edification of his hearers, such as the Book of Psalms and such like.

When the minister who reads shall judge it necessary to expound any part of what is read, let it not be done until the whole chapter or psalm be ended. But regard is always to be had to the time, so that neither preaching nor other ordinances be either constrained or rendered tedious. This rule is to be observed in all other public performances.

Beside public reading of the holy scriptures, every person that can read is to be exhorted to read the scriptures privately (and all others that cannot read, if not disabled by age, or otherwise, are likewise to be exhorted to learn to read) and to have a Bible.[2]

Of Public Prayer before the Sermon

AFTER reading of the Word and singing of the psalm, the minister who is to preach is to endeavour to get his own and his hearers' hearts to be rightly affected with their sins, that they may all mourn because of them before the Lord, and hunger and thirst after the grace of God in Jesus Christ, by proceeding to a more full confession of

2. This paragraph was added by Parliament.

sin, with shame and holy confusion of face, and to call on the Lord to this effect:

To acknowledge our great sinfulness; First, by reason of original sin, which, beside the guilt that makes us liable to everlasting damnation, is the seed of all other sins, has depraved and poisoned all the faculties and powers of soul and body, defiles our best actions, and, were it not restrained, or our hearts renewed by grace, would break forth into innumerable transgressions, and the greatest rebellions against the Lord that ever were committed by the vilest of the sons of men; and next, by reason of actual sins, our own sins, the sins of magistrates, of ministers, and of the whole nation, to which we are many ways accessory: which sins of ours receive many fearful aggravations, we having broken all the commandments of the holy, just, and good law of God, doing that which is forbidden, and leaving undone what is enjoined; and that not only out of ignorance and infirmity, but also more presumptuously, against the light of our minds, checks of our consciences, and motions of his own Holy Spirit to the contrary, so that we have no cloak for our sins; yes, not only despising the riches of God's goodness, forbearance, and long-suffering, but standing out against many invitations and offers of grace in the gospel, not endeavouring, as we ought, to receive Christ into our hearts by faith, or to walk worthy of him in our lives.

To bewail our blindness of mind, hardness of heart, unbelief, impenitency, security [self-confidence], lukewarmness, barrenness; our not endeavouring after mortification and newness of life, nor after the exercise of godliness in the power of it; and that the best of us have not so steadfastly walked with God, kept our garments so unspotted, nor been so zealous of his glory, and the good of others, as we ought; and to mourn over such other sins as the congregation is particularly guilty of, notwithstanding the manifold [many] and great mercies of our God, the love of Christ, the light of the gospel, and reformation of religion, our own purposes, promises, vows, solemn covenant, and other special obligations to the contrary.

To acknowledge and confess that, as we are convinced of our guilt, so, out of a deep sense of it, we judge ourselves unworthy of the smallest benefits, most worthy of God's fiercest wrath, and of all the curses of the law, and heaviest judgments inflicted on the most rebellious sinners; and that he might most justly take his kingdom and gospel from us, plague us with all sorts of spiritual and temporal judgments in this life, and after cast us into utter darkness, in the lake that burns with fire and brimstone, where is weeping and gnashing of teeth for evermore.

Notwithstanding all which, to draw near to the throne of grace, encouraging ourselves with hope of a gracious answer of our prayers, in the riches and all-sufficiency of that only one oblation [offering], the satisfaction and intercession of the Lord Jesus Christ, at the right hand of his Father and our Father; and in confidence of the exceeding great and precious promises of mercy and grace in the new covenant, through the same Mediator of it, to deprecate the heavy wrath and curse of God, which we are not able to avoid, or bear; and humbly and earnestly to supplicate for mercy, in the free and full remission of all our sins, and that only for the bitter sufferings and precious merits of our only Saviour Jesus Christ.

That the Lord would graciously shed abroad his love in our hearts by the Holy Spirit; seal unto us, by the same Spirit of adoption, the full assurance of our pardon and reconciliation; comfort all that mourn in Zion, speak peace to the wounded and troubled spirit, and bind up the broken-hearted: and as for secure and presumptuous sinners, that he would open their eyes, convince their consciences, and turn them from darkness to light, and from the power of Satan to God, that they also may receive forgiveness of sin, and an inheritance among those that are sanctified by faith in Christ Jesus.

With remission of sins through the blood of Christ, to pray for sanctification by his Spirit; the mortification of sin dwelling in and many times tyrannizing over us; the quickening of our dead spirits with the life of God in Christ; grace to fit and enable us for all the duties of life and callings towards God and men; strength against temptations; the sanctified use of blessings and crosses; and perseverance in faith and obedience to the end.

To pray for the propagation of the gospel and kingdom of Christ to all nations; for the conversion of the Jews, the fulness of the Gentiles, the fall of Antichrist, and the hastening of the second coming of our Lord; for the deliverance of the distressed churches abroad from the tyranny of the antichristian faction, and from the cruel oppressions and blasphemies of the Turk; for the blessing of God on the Reformed Churches, especially upon the churches and kingdoms of Scotland, England, and Ireland, now more strictly and religiously united in the Solemn National League and Covenant, and for our plantations in the remote parts of the world; more particularly for that church and kingdom of which we are members, that God would establish peace and truth in it, the purity of all his ordinances, and the power of godliness; prevent and remove heresy, schism, profaneness, superstition, security [self-confidence], and unfruitfulness under the means of grace; heal all our rents and divisions, and preserve us from breach of our Solemn Covenant.

To pray for all in authority, especially for the King's Majesty, that God would make him rich in blessings, both in his person and government, establish his throne in religion and righteousness, save him from evil counsel, and make him a blessed and glorious instrument for the conservation and propagation of the gospel, for the encouragement and protection of them that do well, the terror of all that do evil, and the great good of the whole church, and of all his kingdoms; for the conversion of the Queen, the religious education of the Prince, and the rest of the royal seed; for the comforting of the afflicted Queen of Bohemia, sister to our Sovereign, and for the restitution and establishment of the illustrious Prince Charles, Elector Palatine of the Rhine, to all his dominions and dignities; for a blessing on the High Court of Parliament, when sitting in any of these kingdoms respectively, the nobility, the subordinate judges and magistrates, the gentry, and all the commonality; for all pastors and teachers, that God would fill them with his Spirit, make them exemplarily holy, sober, just, peaceable, and gracious in their lives, sound, faithful, and powerful in their ministry, and follow all their labours with abundance of success and blessing, and give to all his people pastors according to his own heart; for the universities, and all schools and religious seminaries of church and commonwealth, that they may flourish more and more in learning and piety; for the particular city or congregation, that God would pour out a blessing on the ministry of the Word, sacraments, and discipline, on the civil government, and all the several families and persons therein; for mercy to the afflicted under any inward or outward distress; for seasonable weather, and fruitful seasons, as the time may require; for averting the judgments that we either feel or fear, or are liable to as famine, pestilence, the sword, and such like.

And, with confidence of his mercy to his whole church, and the acceptance of our persons, through the merits and mediation of our High Priest, the Lord Jesus, to profess that it is the desire of our souls to have fellowship with God in the reverent and conscionable [conscientious] use of his holy ordinances; and, to that purpose, to pray earnestly for his grace and effectual assistance to the sanctification of his holy sabbath, the Lord's day, in all the duties of it, public and private, both to ourselves, and to all other congregations of his people, according to the riches and excellency of the gospel, this day celebrated and enjoyed.

And because we have been unprofitable hearers in times past, and now cannot of ourselves receive, as we should, the deep things of God, the mysteries of Jesus Christ, which require a spiritual discerning, to pray that the Lord, who teaches to profit, would graciously be pleased to pour out the Spirit of grace, together with the outward means of it, causing us to attain such a measure of the excellency of the knowledge of Christ Jesus our Lord, and, in him, of the things which belong to our peace, that we may account all things but as dross in comparison of him; and that we, tasting the first-fruits of the glory that is to be revealed, may long for a more full and perfect communion with him, that where he is, we may be also, and enjoy the fulness of those joys and pleasures which are at his right hand for evermore.

More particularly, that God would in a special manner furnish his servant (now called to dispense the bread of life to his household) with wisdom, fidelity, zeal, and utterance, that he may divide the Word of God aright, to every one his portion, in evidence and demonstration of the Spirit and power; and that the Lord would circumcise the ears and hearts of the hearers, to hear, love, and receive with meekness the engrafted Word, which is able to save their souls; make them as good ground to receive in the good seed of the Word, and strengthen them against the temptations of Satan, the cares of the world, the hardness of their own hearts, and whatsoever else may hinder their profitable and saving hearing; that so Christ may be so formed in them, and live in them, that all their thoughts may be brought into captivity to the obedience of Christ, and their hearts established in every good word and work for ever.

We judge this to be a convenient order in the ordinary public prayer, yet so, as the minister may defer, as in prudence he shall think fit, some part of these petitions till after his sermon, or offer up to God some of the thanksgivings hereafter appointed, in his prayer before his sermon.

Of the Preaching of the Word

PREACHING of the Word, being the power of God to salvation, and one of the greatest and most excellent works belonging to the ministry of the gospel, should be so performed that the workman need not be ashamed, but may save himself, and those that hear him.

It is presupposed, according to the rules for ordination, that the minister of Christ is in some good measure gifted for so weighty a service by his skill in the original languages, and in such arts and sciences as are handmaids to divinity, by his knowledge in the whole body of theology but most of all in the holy scriptures, having his senses and heart exercised in them above the common [ordinary] sort of believers, and by the illumination of God's Spirit, and other gifts of edification, which, together with reading and studying of the Word, he ought still to seek by prayer and an humble heart, resolving to admit and receive any truth not yet attained, whenever God shall make it known to him. All which he is to make use of, and improve, in his private preparations, before he deliver in public what he has provided.

Ordinarily, the subject of his sermon is to be some text of scripture, holding forth some principle or head of religion, or suitable to some special occasion that has arisen; or he may go on in some chapter, psalm, or book of the holy scripture, as he shall see fit.

Let the introduction to his text be brief and perspicuous [clear], drawn from the text itself, or context, or some parallel place, or general sentence of scripture.

If the text be long, as in histories or parables it sometimes must be, let him give a brief summary of it; if short, a paraphrase of it, if need be: in both, looking diligently to the scope of the text, and pointing at the chief heads and grounds of doctrine which he is to raise from it.

In analysing and dividing his text, he is to regard more the order of matter than of words; and neither to burden the memory of the hearers in the beginning with too many members of division, nor to trouble their minds with obscure terms of art.

In raising doctrines from the text, his care ought to be, First, that the matter be the truth of God. Secondly, that it be a truth contained in or grounded on that text, that the hearers may discern how God teaches it from thence. Thirdly, that he chiefly insist on those doctrines which are principally intended, and make most for the edification of the hearers.

The doctrine is to be expressed in plain terms; or, if anything in it need explaining, it is to be opened, and the consequence also from the text cleared [made clear]. The parallel places of scripture, confirming the doctrine, are rather to be plain and pertinent than many, and, if need be, somewhat insisted upon, and applied to the purpose in hand.

The arguments or reasons are to be solid, and, as much as may be, convincing. The illustrations, of whatever kind, ought to be full of light, and such as may convey the truth into the hearer's heart with spiritual delight.

If any doubt obvious from scripture, reason, or prejudice of the hearers seem to arise, it is very necessary to remove it, by reconciling the seeming differences, answering the reasons, and discovering and taking away the causes of prejudice and mistake. Otherwise it is not fit to detain the hearers with propounding or answering vain or wicked cavils [objections], which, as they are endless, so the propounding and answering of them does more hinder than promote edification.

He is not to rest in general doctrine, although never so much cleared [clarified] and confirmed, but to bring it home to special use, by application to his hearers: which although it prove a work of great difficulty to himself, requiring much prudence, zeal, and meditation, and to the natural and corrupt man will be very unpleasant, yet he is to endeavour to perform it in such a manner, that his hearers may feel the Word of God to be living and powerful, and a discerner of the thoughts and intents of the heart; and that, if any unbeliever or ignorant person be present, he may have the secrets of his heart revealed, and give glory to God.

In the use of instruction or information in the knowledge of some truth, which is a consequence from his doctrine, he may (when convenient) confirm it by a few firm arguments from the text in hand, and other places of scripture, or from the nature of that common-place [common topic] in divinity, of which that truth is a branch.

In confutation of false doctrines, he is neither to raise an old heresy from the grave, nor to mention a blasphemous opinion unnecessarily: but, if the people are in danger of an error, he is to confute it soundly, and endeavour to satisfy their judgments and consciences against all objections.

In exhorting to duties, he is, as he sees cause, to teach also the means that help to the performance of them.

In dehortation [dissuasion], reprehension [rebuke], and public admonition, which require special wisdom, let him, as there shall be cause, not only discover the nature and greatness of the sin, with the misery attending it, but also show the danger his hearers are in to be overtaken and surprised by it, together with the remedies and best way to avoid it.

In applying comfort, whether general, against all temptations, or particular, against some special troubles or terrors, he is carefully to answer such objections as a troubled heart and afflicted spirit may suggest to the contrary. It is also sometimes requisite [necessary] to give some notes of trial (which is very profitable, especially when performed by able and experienced ministers, with circumspection and prudence, and the signs clearly grounded on the holy scripture) whereby the hearers may be able to examine themselves whether they have attained those graces, and performed those duties, to which he exhorts them, or be guilty of the sin rebuked, and in danger of the judgments threatened, or are such to whom the consolations propounded do belong; that accordingly they may be quickened and excited to duty, humbled for their wants and sins, affected with their danger, and strengthened with comfort, as their condition, on examination, shall require.

And, as he does not need always to prosecute every doctrine which lies in his text, so is he wisely to make choice of such uses, as, by his residence and conversing with his flock, he finds most needful and seasonable; and, among these, such as may most draw their souls to Christ, the fountain of light, holiness, and comfort.

This method is not prescribed as necessary for every man, or on every text, but only recommended, as being found by experience to be very much blessed of God, and very helpful for the people's understandings and memories.

But the servant of Christ, whatever his method be, is to perform his whole ministry:

1. Painfully [Painstakingly], not doing the work of the Lord negligently.

2. Plainly, that the meanest [least educated] may understand; delivering the truth not in the enticing words of man's wisdom, but in demonstration of the Spirit and of power, lest the cross of Christ should be made of none effect; abstaining also from an unprofitable use of unknown tongues [languages], strange phrases, and cadences [changes in pitch] of sounds and words; sparingly citing sentences of ecclesiastical or other human writers, ancient or modern, be they never so elegant.

3. Faithfully, looking at the honour of Christ, the conversion, edification, and salvation of the people, not at his own gain or glory; keeping nothing back which may promote those holy ends, giving to every one his own portion, and bearing indifferent [impartial] respect to all, without neglecting the meanest [lowest], or sparing the greatest, in their sins.

4. Wisely, framing all his doctrines, exhortations, and especially his reproofs in such a manner as may be most likely to prevail; showing all due respect to each man's person and place, and not mixing his own passion or bitterness.

5. Gravely, as becomes the Word of God; shunning all such gesture, voice, and expressions as may occasion the corruptions of men to despise him and his ministry.

6. With loving affection, that the people may see all coming from his godly zeal, and hearty desire to do them good. And,

7. As taught of God, and persuaded in his own heart, that all that he teaches is the truth of Christ; and walking before his flock, as an example to them in it; earnestly, both in private and public, recommending his labours to the blessing of God, and watchfully looking to himself, and the flock whereof the Lord has made him overseer. So shall the doctrine of truth be preserved uncorrupt [without corruption], many souls converted and built up, and himself receive manifold [many] comforts of his labours even in this life, and afterward the crown of glory laid up for him in the world to come.

Where there are more ministers in a congregation than one, and they of different gifts, each may more especially apply himself to doctrine or exhortation, according to the gift wherein he most excels, and as they shall agree between themselves.

Of Prayer after Sermon

THE sermon being ended, the minister is *To give thanks for the great love of God, in sending his Son Jesus Christ to us; for the communication of his Holy Spirit; for the light and liberty of the glorious gospel, and the rich and heavenly blessings revealed therein, as namely, election, vocation, adoption, justification, sanctification, and hope of glory; for the admirable goodness of God in freeing the land from antichristian darkness and tyranny, and for all other national deliverances, for the reformation of religion, for the covenant; and for many temporal blessings.*

To pray for the continuance of the gospel, and all ordinances of it, in their purity, power, and liberty.

To turn the chief and most useful heads of the sermon into some few petitions; and to pray that it may abide in the heart, and bring forth fruit.

To pray for preparation for death and judgment, and a watching for the coming of our Lord Jesus Christ.

To entreat of God the forgiveness of the iniquities of our holy things, and the acceptation [acceptance] of our spiritual sacrifice, through the merit and mediation of our great High Priest and Saviour the Lord Jesus Christ.

And because the prayer which Christ taught his disciples is not only a pattern of prayer, but itself a most comprehensive prayer, we recommend it also to be used in the prayers of the church.

And whereas, at the administration of the sacraments, the holding of public fasts and days of thanksgiving and other special occasions, which may afford [produce] matter of special petitions and thanksgivings, it is requisite [necessary] to express somewhat in our public prayers (as at this time it is our duty to pray for a blessing on the Assembly of Divines, the armies by sea and land, for the defence of the King, Parliament, and Kingdom), every minister is herein to apply himself in his prayer, before or after sermon, to those occasions: but, for the manner, he is left to his liberty, as God shall direct and enable him in piety and wisdom to discharge his duty.

The prayer ended, let a psalm be sung, if with convenience it may be done. After which (unless some other ordinance of Christ, that concerns the congregation at that time, be to follow) let the minister dismiss the congregation with a solemn blessing.

Of the Administration of the Sacraments: and first of Baptism

BAPTISM, as it is not unnecessarily to be delayed, so it is not to be administered in any case by any private person, but by a minister of Christ, called to be the steward of the mysteries of God.

Nor is it to be administered in private places, or privately, but in the place of public worship, and in the face of the congregation, where the people may most conveniently see and hear; and not in the places where fonts, in the time of Popery, were unfitly and superstitiously placed.

The child to be baptized, after notice given to the minister the day before, is to be presented by the father, or (in case of his necessary absence) by some Christian friend in his place, professing his earnest desire that the child may be baptized.

Before baptism, the minister is to use some words of instruction, touching the institution, nature, use, and ends of this sacrament, showing,

That it is instituted by our Lord Jesus Christ.

That it is a seal of the covenant of grace, of our engrafting into Christ, and of our union with him, of remission of sins, regeneration, adoption, and life eternal.

That the water in baptism represents and signifies both the blood of Christ, which takes away all guilt of sin, original and actual; and the sanctifying virtue of the Spirit of Christ against the dominion of sin, and the corruption of our sinful nature.

That baptizing, or sprinkling and washing with water, signifies the cleansing from sin by the blood and for the merit of Christ, together with the mortification of sin, and rising from sin to newness of life, by virtue of the death and resurrection of Christ.

That the promise is made to believers and their seed; and that the seed and posterity of the faithful, born within the church, have,

156

by their birth, interest in the covenant, and right to the seal of it, and to the outward privileges of the church under the gospel, no less than the children of Abraham in the time of the Old Testament; the covenant of grace, for substance, being the same; and the grace of God, and the consolation of believers, more plentiful than before.

That the Son of God admitted little children into his presence, embracing and blessing them, saying, For of such is the kingdom of God.

That children, by baptism, are solemnly received into the bosom of the visible church, distinguished from the world and them that are without, and united with believers; and that all who are baptized in the name of Christ do renounce, and by their baptism are bound to fight against, the devil, the world, and the flesh.

That they are Christians, and federally holy before baptism, and therefore are they baptized.

That the inward grace and virtue of baptism is not tied to that very moment of time wherein it is administered; and that the fruit and power of it reaches to the whole course of our life; and that outward baptism is not so necessary that, through the want of it, the infant is in danger of damnation, or the parents guilty, if they do not contemn [despise] or neglect the ordinance of Christ when and where it may be had.

In these or the like instructions, the minister is to use his own liberty and godly wisdom, as the ignorance or errors in the doctrine of baptism, and the edification of the people, shall require.

He is also to admonish all that are present:

To look back to their baptism; to repent of their sins against their covenant with God; to stir up their faith; to improve and make right use of their baptism, and of the covenant sealed thereby betwixt [between] God and their souls.

He is to exhort the parent:

To consider the great mercy of God to him and his child; to bring up the child in the knowledge of the grounds of the Christian religion, and in the nurture and admonition of the Lord; and to let him know the danger of God's wrath to himself and child, if he be negligent: requiring his solemn promise for the performance of his duty.[3]

This being done, prayer is also to be joined with the word of institution, for sanctifying the water to this spiritual use; and the minister is to pray to this or the like effect:

That the Lord, who has not left us as strangers without the covenant of promise, but called us to the privileges of his ordinances, would graciously vouchsafe [condescend] to sanctify and bless his own ordinance of baptism at this time: That he would join the inward baptism of his Spirit with the outward baptism of water; make this baptism to the infant a seal of adoption, remission of sin, regeneration, and eternal life, and all other promises of the covenant of grace: That the child may be planted into the likeness of the death and resurrection of Christ; and that, the body of sin being destroyed in him, he may serve God in newness of life all his days.

Then the minister is to demand the name of the child; which being told him, he is to say, calling the child by his name:

"I baptize thee in[4] the name of the Father, and of the Son, and of the Holy Spirit."

As he pronounces these words, he is to baptize the child with water: which, for the manner of doing of it, is not only lawful but sufficient and most expedient to be by pouring or sprinkling of the water on the face of the child, without adding any other ceremony.

This done, he is to give thanks and pray, to this or the like purpose:

Acknowledging with all thankfulness that the Lord is true and faithful in keeping covenant and mercy.

That he is good and gracious, not only in that he numbers us among his saints, but is pleased also to bestow on our children this singular token and badge of his love in Christ. That, in his truth and special providence, he daily brings some into the bosom of his church, to be partakers of his

---

3. The MSS adds the following (deleted from the final text at the request of the Church of Scotland Assembly in February 1645): "It is recommended to the parent or the Christian friend to make a profession of his faith by answering to these or like questions. Dost thou believe in God the Father, Son and Holy Ghost? Dost thou hold thyself bound to observe all that Christ hath commanded thee, and wilt thou endeavour to so do? Dost thou desire to have this child baptised into the faith and profession of Jesus Christ?"

4. A marginal note in the MSS provided "into" as an alternative, but it appears from the Assembly's own MSS copy to have been dropped, probably by Parliament.

inestimable benefits, purchased by the blood of his dear Son, for the continu-
ance and increase of his church.

And praying:
That the Lord would still continue, and daily confirm more and more,
this his unspeakable favour.

That he would receive the infant now baptized, and solemnly entered into
the household of faith, into his fatherly tuition and defence, and remember
him with the favour that he shows to his people.

That, if he shall be taken out of this life in his infancy, the Lord, who is
rich in mercy, would be pleased to receive him up into glory; and if he live,
and attain the years of discretion, that the Lord would so teach him by his
Word and Spirit, and make his baptism effectual to him, and so uphold
him by his divine power and grace, that by faith he may prevail against
the devil, the world, and the flesh, till in the end he obtain a full and final
victory, and so be kept by the power of God through faith unto salvation,
through Jesus Christ our Lord.

Of the Celebration of the Communion, or Sacrament of the Lord's Supper

THE Communion, or Supper of the Lord, is frequently to be celebrated; but how often may be considered and determined by the ministers, and other church-governors of each congregation, as they shall find most convenient for the comfort and edification of the people committed to their charge. And, when it shall be administered, we judge it convenient to be done after the morning sermon.

The ignorant and the scandalous are not fit to receive the sacrament of the Lord's Supper.[5]

Where this sacrament cannot with convenience be frequently administered, it is requisite [necessary] that public warning be given

5. In lieu of this sentence the original MSS read: "None are to be admitted thereunto but such as being baptized are found upon a full examination by the minister, before the other church officers, to have a competent measure of knowledge, and ability to examine themselves, and do promise their willingness to submit themselves to all the ordinances of Christ, and are of approved conversation [manner of life] according to the rules of Christ. The ignorant, the scandalous, the obstinate are not to be admitted: nor those of another congregation except they bring sufficient testimony." The change was made by Parliament, but the Scottish Church enacted to preserve its earlier practice of examination.

the sabbath-day before the administration of it: and that either then, or on some day of that week, something concerning that ordinance, and the due preparation thereto, and participation of it, be taught; that, by the diligent use of all means sanctified of God to that end, both in public and private, all may come better prepared to that heavenly feast.

When the day is come for administration, the minister, having ended his sermon and prayer, shall make a short exhortation:

Expressing the inestimable benefit we have by this sacrament, together with the ends and use of it: setting forth the great necessity of having our comforts and strength renewed thereby in this our pilgrimage and warfare: how necessary it is that we come to it with knowledge, faith, repentance, love, and with hungering and thirsting souls after Christ and his benefits: how great the danger to eat and drink unworthily.

Next, he is, in the name of Christ, on the one part, to warn all such as are ignorant, scandalous, profane [impious], or that live in any sin or offence against their knowledge or conscience, that they presume not to come to that holy table; showing them that he that eats and drinks unworthily, eats and drinks judgment to himself: and, on the other part, he is in an especial manner to invite and encourage all that labour under the sense of the burden of their sins, and fear of wrath, and desire to reach out to a greater progress in grace than yet they can attain to, to come to the Lord's table; assuring them, in the same name, of ease, refreshing, and strength to their weak and wearied souls.

After this exhortation, warning, and invitation, the table being before decently covered, and so conveniently placed, that the communicants may orderly sit about it, or at it,[6] the minister is to begin the action with sanctifying and blessing the elements of bread and wine set before him (the bread in comely and convenient vessels, so prepared, that, being broken by him, and given, it may be distributed amongst the communicants; the wine also in large cups), having first,

6. The MSS read "about it (or at it as in the Church of Scotland)" so to allow reception in the pew in the English manner ("about it") or "at" the table (as in Scotland). The extra words were omitted in the final text, but the Scots further safeguarded their practice by a supplementary act of their General Assembly.

in a few words, showed that those elements, otherwise common, are now set apart and sanctified to this holy use, by the word of institution and prayer.

Let the words of institution be read out of the Evangelists, or out of the first Epistle of the Apostle Paul to the Corinthians, Chap. 11 verse 23. *I have received of the Lord*, &c. to the 27th Verse, which the minister may, when he sees requisite [necessary], explain and apply.

Let the prayer, thanksgiving, or blessing of the bread and wine be to this effect:

With humble and hearty acknowledgment of the greatness of our misery, from which neither man, nor angel was able to deliver us, and of our great unworthiness of the least of all God's mercies.

To give thanks to God for all his benefits, and especially for that great benefit of our redemption, the love of God the Father, the sufferings and merits of the Lord Jesus Christ the Son of God, by which we are delivered; and for all means of grace, the Word and sacraments; and for this sacrament in particular, by which Christ and all his benefits are applied and sealed up to us, which, notwithstanding the denial of them to others, are in great mercy continued to us, after so much and long abuse of them all.

To profess that there is no other name under heaven by which we can be saved, but the name of Jesus Christ, by whom alone we receive liberty and life, have access to the throne of grace, are admitted to eat and drink at his own table, and are sealed up by his Spirit to an assurance of happiness and everlasting life.

Earnestly to pray to God, the Father of all mercies, and God of all consolation, to vouchsafe [condescend to grant] his gracious presence, and the effectual working of his Spirit in us; and so to sanctify these elements both of bread and wine, and to bless his own ordinance, that we may receive by faith the body and blood of Jesus Christ, crucified for us, and so to feed on him, that he may be one with us, and we one with him; that he may live in us, and we in him, and to him who has loved us, and given himself for us.

All which he is to endeavour to perform with suitable affections [feelings] answerable to such an holy action, and to stir up the like in the people.

The elements being now sanctified by the Word and prayer, the minister, being at the table, is to take the bread in his hand, and say, in these expressions (or other the like, used by Christ or his apostle on this occasion):

"According to the holy institution, command, and example of our blessed Saviour Jesus Christ, I take this bread, and, having given thanks, break it, and give it to you" (there the minister, who is also himself to communicate, is to break the bread, and give it to the communicants); "Take, eat; this is the body of Christ which is broken for you: do this in remembrance of him."

In like manner the minister is to take the cup, and say, in these expressions (or other the like, used by Christ or the apostle on the same occasion):

"According to the institution, command, and example of our Lord Jesus Christ, I take this cup, and give it to you" (here he gives it to the communicants); "This cup is the new testament in the blood of Christ, which is shed for the remission of the sins of many: all of you drink it."

After all have communicated, the minister may, in a few words, put them in mind of the grace of God in Jesus Christ, held forth in this sacrament; and exhort them to walk worthy of it.

The minister is to give solemn thanks to God:

For his rich mercy, and invaluable goodness, vouchsafed [graciously granted] to them in that sacrament; and to entreat for pardon for the defects of the whole service, and for the gracious assistance of his good Spirit, whereby they may be enabled to walk in the strength of that grace, as becomes those who have received so great pledges of salvation.

The collection for the poor is so to be ordered that no part of the public worship be thereby hindered.

Of the Sanctification of the Lord's Day

THE Lord's Day ought to be so remembered beforehand, as that all worldly business of our ordinary callings may be so ordered, and so timely and seasonably laid aside, as they may not be impediments to the due sanctifying of the day when it comes.

The whole day is to be celebrated as holy to the Lord, both in public and private, as being the Christian sabbath. To which end, it is requisite [necessary] that there be a holy cessation or resting all that day from all unnecessary labours; and an abstaining, not only from all sports and pastimes, but also from all worldly words and thoughts.

That the diet [activities] on that day be so ordered [arranged] as that neither servants be unnecessarily detained from the public worship of God, nor any other person hindered from the sanctifying that day. That there be private preparations of every person and family, by prayer for themselves, and for God's assistance of the minister, and for a blessing on his ministry; and by such other holy exercises as may further dispose them to a more comfortable [enjoyable] communion with God in his public ordinances.

That all the people meet so timely [promptly] for public worship that the whole congregation may be present at the beginning, and with one heart solemnly join together in all parts of the public worship, and not depart till after the blessing.

That what time is vacant, between or after the solemn meetings of the congregation in public, be spent in reading, meditation, repetition of sermons; especially by calling their families to an account of what they have heard, and catechising of them, holy conferences, prayer for a blessing on the public ordinances, singing of psalms, visiting the sick, relieving the poor, and such like duties of piety, charity, and mercy, accounting the sabbath a delight.

The Solemnization of Marriage

ALTHOUGH marriage be no sacrament, nor peculiar [exclusive] to the church of God, but common to mankind and of public interest in every commonwealth; yet, because such as marry are to marry in the Lord, and have special need of instruction, direction, and exhortation, from the Word of God, at their entering into such a new condition, and of the blessing of God on them therein, we judge it expedient that marriage be solemnized by a lawful minister of the Word, that he may accordingly counsel them, and pray for a blessing on them.

Marriage is to be betwixt [between] one man and one woman only; and they such as are not within the degrees of consanguinity [blood-relationship] or affinity [relationship through marriage] prohibited by the Word of God; and the parties are to be of years of discretion, fit to make their own choice, or, on good grounds, to give their mutual consent.

Before the solemnizing of marriage between any persons, the purpose [intent] of marriage shall be published by the minister three several [distinct] sabbath-days, in the congregation, at the place or places of their most usual and constant abode, respectively. And of this publication the minister who is to join them in marriage shall have sufficient testimony, before he proceed to solemnize the marriage.

Before that publication of such their purpose [intent], if the parties be under age the consent of the parents, or others under whose power they are, in case the parents be dead, is to be made known to the church officers of that congregation, to be recorded. The like is to be observed in the proceedings of all others, although of age, whose parents are living, for their first marriage. And, in after marriages of either of those parties, they shall be exhorted not to contract marriage without first acquainting their parents with it (if with convenience it may be done), endeavouring to obtain their consent. Parents ought not to force their children to marry without their free consent, nor deny their own consent without just cause.

After the purpose or contract of marriage has been thus published, the marriage is not to be long deferred. Therefore the minister, having had convenient warning, and nothing being objected to hinder it, is publicly to solemnize it in the place appointed by authority for public worship,[7] before a competent number of credible witnesses, at some convenient hour of the day, at any time of the year, except on a day of public humiliation. And we advise that it be not on the Lord's day.

And because all relations are sanctified by the Word and prayer, the minister is to pray for a blessing on them, to this effect:

Acknowledging our sins, whereby we have made ourselves less than the least of all the mercies of God, and provoked him to embitter all our comforts; earnestly, in the name of Christ, to entreat the Lord (whose presence and favour is the happiness of every condition, and sweetens every relation) to be their portion, and to own and accept them in Christ, who

7. The original MSS read "in the place of the public meeting of that congregation" but was changed by Parliament at the request of the Church of Scotland.

are now to be joined in the honourable estate of marriage, the covenant of their God. And that, as he has brought them together by his providence, he would sanctify them by his Spirit, giving them a new frame of heart fit for their new estate; enriching them with all graces whereby they may perform the duties, enjoy the comforts, undergo the cares, and resist the temptations which accompany that condition, as becomes Christians.

The prayer being ended, it is convenient that the minister do briefly declare to them out of the scripture:

The institution, use, and ends of marriage, with the conjugal duties, which, in all faithfulness, they are to perform each to other; exhorting them to study the holy Word of God, that they may learn to live by faith, and to be content in the midst of all marriage cares and troubles, sanctifying God's name, in a thankful, sober, and holy use of all conjugal comforts; praying much with and for one another; watching over and provoking each other to love and good works; and to live together as the heirs of the grace of life.

After solemn charging of the persons to be married, before the great God, who searches all hearts, and to whom they must give a strict account at the last day, that if either of them know any cause, by pre-contract or otherwise, why they may not lawfully proceed to marriage, that they now discover [disclose] it, the minister (if no impediment be acknowledged) shall cause first the man to take the woman by the right hand, saying these words:

"I N. do take thee N. to be my married wife, and do, in the presence of God, and before this congregation, promise and covenant to be a loving and faithful husband to thee, until God shall separate us by death."

Then the woman shall take the man by the right hand, and say these words:

"I N. do take thee N. to be my married husband, and I do, in the presence of God, and before this congregation, promise and covenant to be a loving, faithful, and obedient wife to thee, until God shall separate us by death."

Then, without any further ceremony, the minister shall, in the face of the congregation, pronounce them to be husband and wife, according to God's ordinance, and so conclude the action with prayer to this effect:

That the Lord would be pleased to accompany his own ordinance with his blessing, beseeching him to enrich the persons now married, as with other pledges of his love, so particularly with the comforts and fruits of marriage, to the praise of his abundant mercy, in and through Christ Jesus.

A register is to be carefully kept, wherein the names of the parties so married, with the time of their marriage, are forthwith to be fairly recorded in a book provided for that purpose, for the perusal of all whom it may concern.[8]

Concerning Visitation of the Sick

IT is the duty of the minister not only to teach the people committed to his charge in public, but privately; and particularly to admonish, exhort, reprove, and comfort them, on all seasonable [appropriate] occasions, so far as his time, strength, and personal safety will permit.

He is to admonish them, in time of health, to prepare for death; and, for that purpose, they are often to confer with their minister about the estate of their souls; and, in times of sickness, to desire [seek] his advice and help, timely [promptly] and seasonably [appropriately], before their strength and understanding fail them.

Times of sickness and affliction are special opportunities put into his hand by God to minister a word in season to weary souls: because then the consciences of men are or should be more awakened to bethink themselves of [think on] their spiritual estate for eternity; and Satan also takes advantage then to load them more with sore and heavy temptations: therefore the minister, being sent for, and repairing [going] to the sick, is to apply himself, with all tenderness and love, to administer some spiritual good to his soul, to this effect.

He may, from the consideration of the present sickness, instruct him out of scripture, that diseases come not by chance, or by distem-

---

8. The MSS adds: "It is likewise humbly proposed to both the honourable Houses of Parliament to pray them to consider of some law for prevention of children marrying without their parents' consent, and of parents forcing or denying of marriage to their children unjustly, and of ministers presuming to join in marriage any persons without such due consent." Understandably, this was omitted from the published text.

pers [disorders] of body only, but by the wise and orderly guidance of the good hand of God to every particular person smitten by them. And that, whether it be laid on him out of displeasure for sin, for his correction and amendment, or for trial and exercise of his graces, or for other special and excellent ends, all his sufferings shall turn to his profit, and work together for his good, if he sincerely labour to make a sanctified use of God's visitation, neither despising his chastening, nor waxing [growing] weary of his correction.

If he suspect him of ignorance, he shall examine him in the principles of religion, especially touching repentance and faith; and, as he sees cause, instruct him in the nature, use, excellency, and necessity of those graces; as also touching the covenant of grace; and Christ the Son of God, the Mediator of it; and concerning remission of sins by faith in him.

He shall exhort the sick person to examine himself, to search and try his former ways and his estate towards God. And if the sick person shall declare any scruple, doubt, or temptation that are on him, instructions and resolutions shall be given to satisfy and settle him.[9]

If it appear that he has not a due sense of his sins, endeavours ought to be used[10] to convince him of his sins, of the guilt and desert of them; of the filth and pollution which the soul contracts by them; and of the curse of the law, and wrath of God, due to them; that he may be truly affected with and humbled for them, and withal [as well] to make known[11] the danger of deferring repentance, and of neglecting salvation at any time offered, to awaken[12] his conscience, and rouse him

---

9. In the original MSS this paragraph read: "He shall require the sick person to examine himself, to search and try his former ways and his estate before God; exhorting him to declare what burden or trouble lies upon his conscience, what sense he hath of his sins, what scruples, doubts, temptations are upon him; and shall accordingly instruct and relieve him. If the minister be unacquainted with his condition, he shall inquire of it, and what communion he hath held with God in his public ordinances, how he has prized the Gospel and means of grace, what care he hath had of private duties, and of keeping a conscience void of offence toward God and man, and what evidence or hopes he hath gotten of the pardon of his sins and his peace with God."

10. In the original MSS the preceding words read: "If he find he hath not walked as becometh the Gospel, he shall endeavour."

11. The original MSS has "letting him know" in lieu of "and withal to make known."

12. The original MSS has "thereby awakening" in lieu of "to awaken."

up out of a stupid and secure [self-confident] condition, to apprehend [recognise] the justice and wrath of God, before whom none can stand, but he that, lost in himself, lays hold on Christ by faith.

If he has endeavoured to walk in the ways of holiness, and to serve God in uprightness, although not without many failings and infirmities; or, if his spirit be broken with the sense of sin, or cast down through want of the sense of God's favour; then it will be fit to raise him up, by setting before him the freeness and fulness of God's grace, the sufficiency of righteousness in Christ, the gracious offers in the gospel, that all who repent and believe with all their heart in God's mercy through Christ, renouncing their own righteousness, shall have life and salvation in him.

It may be also useful to show him that death has in it no spiritual evil to be feared by those that are in Christ, because sin, the sting of death, is taken away by Christ,[13] who has delivered all that are his from the bondage of the fear of death, triumphed over the grave, given us victory, is himself entered into glory to prepare a place for his people: so that neither life nor death shall be able to separate them from God's love in Christ, in whom such are sure, though now they must be laid in the dust, to obtain a joyful and glorious resurrection to eternal life.

Advice also may be given,[14] as to beware of an ill-grounded persuasion of mercy, or of the goodness of his condition for heaven, so to disclaim all merit in himself, and to cast himself wholly on God for mercy, in the sole merits and mediation of Jesus Christ, who has engaged [committed] himself never to cast off them who in truth and sincerity come unto him. Care also must be taken that the sick person be not cast down into despair,[15] by such a severe representation of the wrath of God due to him for his sins, as is not mollified by a

13. The original MSS reads the sentence to here: "He shall further endeavour to strengthen the sick person so qualified against the fear of death, as having in it no spiritual evil to be feared by those who are in Christ, because sin, and the sting of death is taken away by Christ."

14. In the original MSS the sentence to here reads: "If weakness disable the sick person from giving clear expressions of his repentance and obedience to the Gospel, the minister shall with all prudence and direction advise him."

15. In the original MSS the sentence to here reads: "The minister is also to take care that he cast him not down into despair."

seasonable propounding [appropriate setting forth] of Christ and his merit for a door of hope to every penitent believer.

When the sick person is best composed [calm and settled], may be least disturbed, and other necessary offices [duties] about him least hindered, the minister, if desired [requested], shall pray with him, and for him, to this effect:

Confessing and bewailing of sin original and actual; the miserable condition of all by nature, as being children of wrath, and under the curse; acknowledging that all diseases, sicknesses, death, and hell itself are the proper issues and effects of it; imploring God's mercy for the sick person, through the blood of Christ; beseeching that God would open his eyes, discover to him his sins, cause him to see himself lost in himself, make known to him the cause why God smites him, reveal Jesus Christ to his soul for righteousness and life, give to him his Holy Spirit, to create and strengthen faith to lay hold on Christ, to work in him comfortable evidences of his love, to arm him against temptations, to take off his heart from the world, to sanctify his present visitation, to furnish him with patience and strength to bear it, and to give him perseverance in faith to the end.

That, if God shall please to add to his days, he would vouchsafe [condescend] to bless and sanctify all means of his recovery; to remove the disease, renew his strength, and enable him to walk worthy of God, by a faithful remembrance and diligent observing of such vows and promises of holiness and obedience as men are apt to make in times of sickness, that he may glorify God in the remaining part of his life.

And, if God have determined to finish his days by the present visitation, he may find such evidence of the pardon of all his sins, of his interest in Christ, and eternal life by Christ as may cause his inward man to be renewed, while his outward man decays; that he may behold death without fear, cast himself wholly on Christ without doubting, desire to be dissolved and to be with Christ, and so receive the end of his faith, the salvation of his soul, through the only merits and intercession of the Lord Jesus Christ, our alone Saviour and all-sufficient Redeemer.

The minister shall admonish him also (as there shall be cause) to set his house in order, thereby to prevent inconveniences [difficulties]; to take care for payment of his debts, and to make restitution or satisfaction where he has done any wrong; to be reconciled to those with

169

whom he has been at variance, and fully to forgive all men their trespasses against him, as he expects forgiveness at the hand of God.

Lastly, the minister may improve the present occasion to exhort those about the sick person to consider their own mortality, to return to the Lord, and make peace with him; in health to prepare for sickness, death, and judgment; and all the days of their appointed time so to wait until their change come, that when Christ, who is our life, shall appear, they may appear with him in glory.

Concerning Burial of the Dead

WHEN any person departs this life, let the dead body, on the day of burial, be decently attended from the house to the place appointed for public burial, and there immediately interred, without any ceremony.

And because the custom of kneeling down, and praying by or towards the dead corpse, and other such usages, in the place where it lies before it be carried to burial, are superstitious; and for that praying, reading, and singing, both in going to and at the grave, have been grossly abused, are no way beneficial to the dead, and have proved many ways hurtful to the living; therefore let all such things be laid aside.

Howbeit, we judge it very convenient that the Christian friends, which accompany the dead body to the place appointed for public burial, do apply themselves to meditations and conferences suitable to the occasion and that the minister, as on other occasions, so at this time, if he be present, may put them in remembrance of their duty.

That this shall not extend to deny any civil respects or deferences [courtesies] at the burial, suitable to the rank and condition of the party deceased, while he was living.

Concerning Public Solemn Fasting

WHEN some great and notable judgments are either inflicted on a people, or apparently imminent, or by some extraordinary provocations notoriously deserved; as also when some special blessing is to be sought and obtained, public solemn fasting (which is to continue the whole day) is a duty that God expects from that nation or people.

A religious fast requires total abstinence, not only from all food (unless bodily weakness do manifestly [clearly] disable from holding out till the fast be ended, in which case somewhat may be taken, yet very sparingly, to support nature, when ready to faint), but also from all worldly labour, discourses, and thoughts, and from all bodily delights, and such like (although at other times lawful), rich apparel, ornaments, and such like, during the fast; and much more from whatever is in the nature or use scandalous and offensive, as gaudish [showy] attire, lascivious habits and gestures, and other vanities of either sex; which we recommend to all ministers, in their places, diligently and zealously to reprove, as at other times, so especially at a fast, without respect of persons, as there shall be occasion.

Before the public meeting, each family and person apart are privately to use all religious care to prepare their hearts to such a solemn work, and to be early at the congregation.

So large a portion of the day as conveniently may be is to be spent in public reading and preaching of the Word, with singing of psalms, fit to quicken affections [feelings] suitable to such a duty: but especially in prayer, to this or the like effect:

Giving glory to the great Majesty of God, the Creator, Preserver, and supreme Ruler of all the world, the better to affect us thereby with an holy reverence and awe of him; acknowledging his manifold [many] great and tender mercies, especially to the church and nation, the more effectually to soften and abase our hearts before him; humbly confessing of sins of all sorts, with their several aggravations; justifying God's righteous judgments, as being far less than our sins do deserve; yet humbly and earnestly imploring his mercy and grace for ourselves, the church and nation, for our king and all in authority, and for all others for whom we are bound to pray (according as the present exigency requires), with more special importunity and enlargement than at other times; applying by faith the promises and goodness of God for pardon, help, and deliverance from the evils felt, feared, or deserved; and for obtaining the blessings which we need and expect; together with a giving up of ourselves wholly and for ever to the Lord.

In all these, the ministers, who are the mouths of the people to God, ought so to speak from their hearts, on serious and thorough premeditation of them, that both themselves and their people may be much affected, and even melted thereby, especially with sorrow for their sins; that it may be indeed a day of deep humiliation and afflicting of the soul.

Special choice is to be made of such scriptures to be read, and of such texts for preaching, as may best work the hearts of the hearers to the special business of the day, and most dispose them to humiliation and repentance: insisting most on those particulars which each minister's observation and experience tells him are most conducing to the edification and reformation of that congregation to which he preaches.

Before the close of the public duties, the minister is, in his own and the people's name, to engage his and their hearts to be the Lord's, with professed purpose and resolution to reform whatever is amiss among them, and more particularly such sins as they have been more remarkably guilty of; and to draw near to God, and to walk more closely and faithfully with him in new obedience than ever before.

He is also to admonish the people, with all importunity [persistent urgency], that the work of that day does not end with the public duties of it, but that they are so to improve the remainder of the day, and of their whole life, in reinforcing on themselves and their families in private all those godly affections [feelings] and resolutions which they professed in public, as that they may be settled in their hearts for ever, and themselves may more sensibly [consciously] find that God has smelt a sweet savour in Christ from their performances, and is pacified towards them, by answers of grace, in pardoning of sin, in removing of judgments, in averting or preventing of plagues, and in conferring of blessings, suitable to the conditions and prayers of his people, by Jesus Christ.

Besides solemn and general fasts enjoined by authority, we judge that at other times congregations may keep days of fasting as divine providence shall administer to them special occasion; and also that families may do the same, so it be not on days wherein the congregation to which they do belong is to meet for fasting, or other public duties of worship.

Concerning the Observation of Days of Public Thanksgiving

WHEN any such day is to be kept, let notice be given of it, and of the occasion of it, some convenient time before, that the people may the better prepare themselves thereto.

The day being come, and the congregation (after private preparations) being assembled, the minister is to begin with a word of exhortation, to stir up the people to the duty for which they are met, and with a short prayer for God's assistance and blessing (as at other conventions for public worship), according to the particular occasion of their meeting.

Let him then make some pithy narration of the deliverance obtained, or mercy received, or of whatever has occasioned that assembling of the congregation, that all may better understand it, or be minded of it, and more affected with it.

And, because singing of psalms is of all other the most proper ordinance for expressing of joy and thanksgiving, let some pertinent psalm or psalms be sung for that purpose, before or after the reading of some portion of the Word suitable to the present business.

Then let the minister who is to preach proceed to further exhortation and prayer before his sermon, with special reference to the present work: after which, let him preach on some text of Scripture pertinent to the occasion.

The sermon ended, let him not only pray, as at other times after preaching is directed, with remembrance of the necessities of the Church, King, and State, if before the sermon they were omitted, but enlarge himself in due and solemn thanksgiving for former mercies and deliverances; but more especially for that which at the present calls them together to give thanks: with humble petition for the continuance and renewing of God's wonted [accustomed] mercies, as need shall be, and for sanctifying grace to make a right use of it. And so, having sung another psalm, suitable to the mercy, let him dismiss the congregation with a blessing, that they may have some convenient time for their repast and refreshing.

But the minister, before their dismission [dismissal], is solemnly to admonish them to beware of all excess and riot [revelry], tending to gluttony or drunkenness, and much more of these sins themselves, in their eating and refreshing; and to take care that their mirth and rejoicing be not carnal, but spiritual, which may make God's praise to be glorious, and themselves humble and sober; and that both their feeding and rejoicing may render them more cheerful and enlarged, further to celebrate his praises in the midst of the congregation, when they return to it in the remaining part of that day.

When the congregation shall be again assembled, the like course in praying, reading, preaching, singing of psalms, and offering up of more praise and thanksgiving, that is before directed for the morning, is to be renewed and continued, so far as the time will give leave.

At one or both of the public meetings that day, a collection is to be made for the poor (and in the like manner on the day of public humiliation), that their loins[16] may bless us, and rejoice the more with us. And the people are to be exhorted at the end of the latter meeting to spend the residue of that day in holy duties and testifications [testifyings] of Christian love and charity one towards another, and of rejoicing more and more in the Lord, as becomes those who make the joy of the Lord their strength.

Of Singing of Psalms

IT is the duty of Christians to praise God publicly, by singing of psalms together in the congregation, and also privately in the family.

In singing of psalms, the voice is to be tunably and gravely ordered; but the chief care must be to sing with understanding and with grace in the heart, making melody to the Lord.

That the whole congregation may join herein, every one that can read is to have a psalm book; and all others, not disabled by age or otherwise, are to be exhorted to learn to read. But for the present, where many in the congregation cannot read, it is convenient that the minister, or some other fit person appointed by him and the other ruling officers, do read the psalm, line by line, before the singing of it.

---

16. It appears that "loins" is used here for the person who is strengthened/protected by the gifts received.

AN APPENDIX, Touching Days and Places for Public Worship

THERE is no day commanded in scripture to be kept holy under the gospel but the Lord's day, which is the Christian Sabbath.

Festival days, vulgarly called *Holy-days*, having no warrant in the Word of God, are not to be continued.

Nevertheless, it is lawful and necessary, on special emergent occasions, to separate a day or days for public fasting or thanksgiving, as the several eminent and extraordinary dispensations of God's providence shall administer cause and opportunity to his people.

As no place is capable of any holiness, under pretence of whatsoever dedication or consecration, so neither is it subject to such pollution by any superstition formerly used, and now laid aside, as may render it unlawful or inconvenient for Christians to meet together therein for the public worship of God. And therefore we hold it requisite [necessary] that the places of public assembling for worship among us should be continued and employed to that use.

Index of Subjects and Names

177